AQA

GCSE Modern World History

Revision Guide

Second Edition

David Ferriby, Steve Waugh
and **Ben Walsh**

HODDER
EDUCATION
AN HACHETTE UK COMPANY

Acknowledgements

The Publishers would like to thank the following for permission to reproduce copyright material:

Photo credits
p.10 © Henry Guttmann/Getty Images; **p.27** © Reproduced with permission of Punch Ltd, www.punch.co.uk; **p.52** © Popperfoto/Getty Images; **p.93** © Culver Pictures; **pp.101 & 102** © David King Collection; **p.108** © The Wiener Library; **p.110** Courtesy The British Cartoon Archive, University of Kent © Evening Standard/Solo Syndication; **p.121** © Bettmann/Corbis; **p.123** © The Granger Collection, NYC/TopFoto **p.134** © Buyenlarge/Getty Images; **p.143** © Topham Picturepoint/TopFoto; **p.145** *both* © Bettmann/Corbis.

Every effort has been made to contact copyright holders, and the publishers apologise for any omissions which they will be pleased to rectify at the earliest opportunity.

Although every effort has been made to ensure that website addresses are correct at time of going to press, Hodder Education cannot be held responsible for the content of any website mentioned in this book. It is sometimes possible to find a relocated web page by typing in the address of the home page for a website in the URL window of your browser.

Hachette UK's policy is to use papers that are natural, renewable and recyclable products and made from wood grown in sustainable forests. The logging and manufacturing processes are expected to conform to the environmental regulations of the country of origin.

Orders: please contact Bookpoint Ltd, 130 Milton Park, Abingdon, Oxon OX14 4SB. Telephone: (44) 01235 827720. Fax: (44) 01235 400454. Lines are open 9.00–5.00, Monday to Saturday, with a 24-hour message-answering service. Visit our website at www.hoddereducation.co.uk.

© David Ferriby, Steve Waugh and Ben Walsh, 2014

First published in 2010 by Hodder Education,
An Hachette UK company,
338 Euston Road,
London NW1 3BH
This second edition published 2014

Impression number   10 9 8 7 6 5 4 3 2
Year   2016 2015

Cover photo: President Nixon with helmeted soldiers, 1969 © Bettmann/CORBIS
Illustrations by Barking Dog Art, Peter Lubach and Phoenix Photosetting
Typeset by Integra Software Services Pvt. Ltd., Pondicherry, India
Printed in Spain

A catalogue record for this title is available from the British Library

ISBN: 978 1471 831 751

Contents

How to use this book

Key issues (beginning of chapter)

The key issues are what the examiners will have in mind when they are setting questions. The exams would never ask you to 'write everything you know about X or Y', they always have an angle. These key issues are 'the angle'. The reason for learning the rest of the facts is so that you can answer questions about these key issues. The content follows exactly what the AQA specification says about those key issues.

Explanation and Comment

The main text explains all the content clearly and the Comment boxes provide extra information to put events in context or highlight other issues that you should be aware of.

Key terms

These boxes help you to learn the essential vocabulary by providing you with difficult or new words and giving a definition of their meaning. These are specialist terms that might be used in an exam without any explanation so you need to be able to understand them and use them confidently in your own writing. You could make your own glossary in your notebook.

Revision task

Use these tasks to make sure you have understood every topic and to help you record the key information about each topic. These tasks help you to think about the content rather than simply read it.

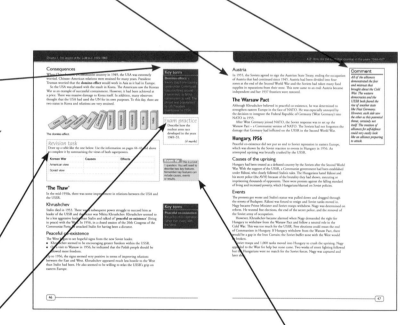

Exam practice

These boxes provide sample exam questions for each topic. You can check your answers against sample answers online at www.hodderplus.co.uk/modernworldhistory to help to improve your grades.

Exam tip

These tips accompany the Exam practice questions. They give you extra tips on how to answer the questions successfully in order to get the best grades possible.

Key content (end of chapter)

This is a revision checklist. Be sure you know about each term or phrase in this key content summary. You can also check your knowledge of each topic with our free 'quick quizzes' which you can find online at www.hodderplus.co.uk/modernworldhistory.

Introduction

You will soon be taking your GCSE in Modern World History. Your aim is to get the best grade that you can. Our aim in this book is to help you get that grade.

To improve your grade you need to:
- get organised – this book will help you make a revision plan and stick to it
- know the content – this book will help you learn the core content for your course
- apply your knowledge – this book will help you apply what you know to actual examination questions.

How to revise

There is no single way to revise, but there are some golden rules everyone should follow.

1 *Know the objectives of your course*
   Ask your teacher for full details of the course you are taking. This book is geared to the AQA Modern World syllabus.

2 *Make a revision plan and stick to it*
   Start your revision early – the earlier the better. Revise regularly – regular, short spells are better than panicky six-hour slogs until 2a.m.

3 *Revise actively*
   Be a scribbler; make notes as you learn. You will need an exercise book for most of the revision tasks but you can also write in this book.

The rest of this introduction is about how to apply these rules to your revision and make sure that you get the grade you are aiming for.

1. Know the objectives of your course

Assessment objectives in GCSE History

1 *Recall, select and communicate knowledge and understanding of history*
   You have to know things, and be able to explain what you know in a way that shows you understand what you are writing. This means:
- using your knowledge of a topic to back up what you say in your answer
- organising this knowledge to answer the question set.

2 *Demonstrate understanding of the past through explanation and analysis of …*
- *key concepts: causation, consequence, continuity, change and significance within a historical context*
- *key features and characteristics of the periods studied and the relationship between them.*

   This means organising your answer in order to:
- show the ability to analyse when this is asked for, rather than to describe
- show understanding of causation, etc.

3 *Understand, analyse and evaluate:*
   (a) a range of source material as part of a historical enquiry
   This means using any kind of material, including photographs, diaries, books, recorded interviews and films from the period you are studying.

   You are expected to:
- be able to select important information from the source
- interpret what is being said and make inferences
- decide how useful or reliable the source is to a historian.

(b) how aspects of the past have been interpreted and represented in different ways as part of a historical enquiry
This means that you have to be able to analyse and interpret how and why historical events, people and situations have been interpreted and represented in different ways.

You are expected to:
- decide how fair or accurate an interpretation is
- compare different interpretations of an event.

In all this, remember that the examiner is interested in seeing how much you can think for yourself and apply your knowledge and understanding to the question set.

2. Make a revision plan

You not only need to plan your revision for History, but you need to fit it in with your revision for all your other GCSE subjects.

You could use this table to plan your overall revision.

Dates		Revision targets and deadlines			
Month	Week	History	Science	English	Others
Jan	4	Key points summary card for Russia			
Feb	2		Tests on metals		
Mar				Controlled Assessment session	

You could then construct a table like the one below to plan your History revision. In your plan, aim to come back to each topic several times so that you revise in stages.

Stage 1: Put the date normal school-based work on a topic will be/was completed.
Stage 2: Put the target date for finishing your own summary of the key points for each topic.
Stage 3: Decide when you will give yourself memory tests.
Stage 4: Schedule time for fine-tuning your revision (for example, final memorising and/or practice examination questions).

History topics	Date	Key points summary	Memory test	Fine tuning
1 Versailles		March	April	Specimen Paper
2 League of Nations				
3				

3. Revise actively

When faced with revising for GCSE History, most students say:

The ideas in this book are aimed at helping you to remember the core content.

Use the revision tasks in this book

The best way to remember information is to use it – to revise actively. To take an everyday example: to start with it is difficult to remember a new telephone number, but the more you use it the easier it is to remember it.

Throughout this book, you will find revision tasks. Don't miss them out. If you do the tasks you will have to use the information in the book. If you use the information you will remember it better. The more you use the information the better you will remember it.

Use the 'key words' method

Think of your brain as a computer. To read a file on a computer, you need to know the name of the file. The file name is the key, and if you do not have this key you cannot get to the file, even though the computer has the file in its memory.

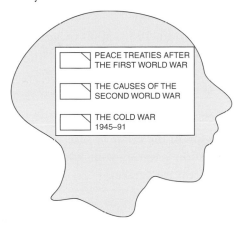

Your brain works in a similar way. When you read something it goes in, but to get the information out again you need the key to unlock your memory. So one way to jog your memory is to use a 'key words' method. This is how it works.

1   As you read through each paragraph, highlight one or two key words. For example, when answering the question:

'What were the main political and economic features of the USA during the 1920s?'

● It had a *democratic system of government*. The President and Congress of the USA were chosen in free democratic elections.

● It had a *capitalist economy*. Business and property were privately owned. Individuals could make profits in business or move jobs if they wished. However, they might also go bankrupt or lose their jobs.

● The USA was the world's wealthiest country, but under capitalism there were always *great contrasts* – some people were very rich, others were very poor.

2   You can then use cue cards, or the key content list at the end of each chapter, to summarise your key words for each subheading. In this way, you can summarise a whole topic on one sheet.

3   Later on, return to your revision plan and recall or rewrite important paragraphs using just the key words to jog your memory.

Other revision ideas

Different people revise in different ways and you may have your own ideas on how to work. Here are some other techniques that students have used.

● summarising events in diagrams or pictures
● making a recording of the text and playing it back
● using acronyms or mnemonics
● working with friends:
  – testing each other
  – comparing your answers to practice questions.

How to answer exam questions

Unit 1 of the examination

Chapters 1–6 cover what is included in the examination for **Unit 1** on **International Relations in the Twentieth Century**.

In the examination, you will only be answering questions on THREE of these six chapters. Make sure that you only revise the chapters that cover what you have studied!

NB If you are only entered for the Short Course GCSE exam, you need only answer questions on TWO chapters.

1 The origins of the First World War (pages 8–17)
2 Peacemaking 1918–1919 and the League of Nations (pages 18–27)
3 Hitler's foreign policy and the origins of the Second World War (pages 28–35)
4 The origins of the Cold War, 1945–1960 (pages 36–49)
5 Crises of the Cold War and Détente, 1960–1980 (pages 50–58)
6 The collapse of Communism and the Post-Cold War World, 1980–2000 (pages 59–65)

In the examination, there is one set of three questions on each of the six chapters. The three questions will always be of the same types and appear in the same order:

- **Description of key features and characteristics**

  For example, 'Describe the Nazi-Soviet Pact of August 1939.'   *4 marks*

When answering this type of question, stick to description of the event or situation. Do NOT be tempted to analyse or give reasons. This is not required. The question is testing your knowledge only.

For a high mark, the examiner will be looking for descriptive details.

- **Source (written or visual) requiring analysis and evaluation**

  For example, 'Do you agree with Source A that lack of interest in the Sudetenland was the main reason that the Munich Agreement of September 1938 was signed? Explain your answer by referring to the purpose of the source, as well as using its content and your own knowledge.'   *6 marks*

When answering this type of question, you need to consider whether you agree or disagree – or whether your view is a mixture of both; that is, the source has uses, but it also has limitations. You need then to consider these uses and limitations in terms of:

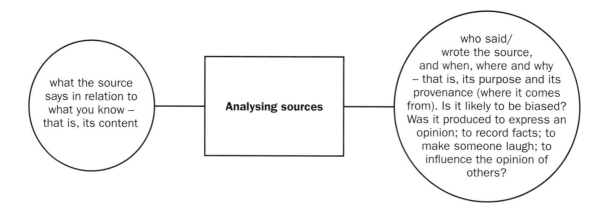

Do not assume that a source produced at the time is necessarily more useful than one produced later, or vice versa. Take each source on its merits.

In all aspects of the answer, try to develop your ideas by explaining them fully, and/or giving factual details. This will enable you to reach a high level.

A word of warning on limitations: do not include impossible limitations. If the source is a photograph of an event, do not say that the source is limited because it misses out all factual details. Concentrate on the way in which the source might be limited in terms of what it is – not what it isn't.

● **Longer-answer question requiring analysis**   *10 marks*

This kind of question will ask you to analyse which of two events or situations listed was more important, for example, in causing something to happen.

For example, 'Which was more important as a reason for the development of the Cold War in the years 1948 to 1955:
- the Berlin Blockade, 1948–1949
- the Korean War, 1950–1953?

You must refer to **both** reasons when explaining your answer.'

The important thing here is to concentrate on ANALYSIS – that is, explaining WHY each event or situation contributed to the Cold War. Do NOT waste your time in the exam DESCRIBING each event. That will only get you a maximum of level 2 (3–5 marks).

Ideally, write a paragraph giving reasons why one was important, then a second paragraph for the other, and then a third paragraph giving a conclusion, and assessing which was more important – with clear reasoning.

Unit 2 of the examination

Chapters 7–14 cover the eight most popular topics in the examination for **Unit 2** on **Twentieth-Century Depth Studies**.

In the examination you need to answer the questions from any ONE topic in Section A, ONE topic in Section B and ONE topic in Section C. (Not all three can be on the USA.). Make sure that you only revise the chapters that cover what you have studied!

SECTION A
7   From Tsardom to Communism: Russia, 1914–1924 (pages 66–76)
8   Weimar Germany, 1919–1929 (pages 77–85)
9   The Roaring '20s: USA, 1919–1929 (pages 86–95)

SECTION B
10   Stalin's dictatorship: USSR, 1924–1941 (pages 96–105)
11   Hitler's Germany, 1929–1945 (pages 106–119)
12   Depression and the New Deal: USA, 1929–1941 (pages 120–128)

SECTION C
13   Race relations in the USA, 1945–1968 (pages 129–138)
14   War in Vietnam, 1954–1975 (pages 139–148)

The other two topics on the question paper are not covered in this book. They are:
- Britain: the challenge in Northern Ireland, 1960–1999
- The Middle East, 1956–1999.

Unit 2 – Section A

There is a set of three questions on each of the three topics. Remember that you have only to answer the three questions on ONE topic.

The three questions on each topic will always be of the same types and appear in the same order:

● **Comprehension and deduction**   *4 marks*

For example, 'What does Source A suggest about the reasons for the introduction of War Communism in Russia in 1918?'

When answering this type of question, stick to what is asked. Do NOT include your own knowledge on the subject.

All you have to do is to show that you have understood what is in the source. You can get two marks for just saying what is in the source.

The other two marks require you to show understanding and make a deduction or inference – for example, explaining what the source is hinting at. The answer does not have to be more than a few lines long.

- **Analysis (e.g. causation) using your knowledge** *6 marks*

  For example, 'Explain why African Americans hated the Ku Klux Klan in the USA in the 1920s.'

What is needed here is NOT description, but reasoning. To get a high mark, you need to explain two or more reasons with relevant details. It is in providing the details that you can use your knowledge.

Preferably set out your answer in two or three paragraphs.

- **Utility: Analysing how useful a source is** *10 marks*

  For example, 'How useful is Source D for studying hyperinflation in Germany in 1923? Use Source D and your knowledge to explain your answer.'

You need to discuss the uses and limitations of the source in terms of:

- content
- analysis of the provenance (as explained on page 4).

Do not assume that a source produced at the time is necessarily more useful than one produced later, or vice versa. Take each source on its merits.

Do not waste time at the start of your answer describing the content of the source. This part of your answer can only reach level 1.

In the exam, you might find it useful to plan ideas quickly by drawing a rough grid:

Reasons why the source is useful – using your knowledge.	Reasons why the source is limited in use – using your knowledge.
Reasons why the source is useful – by looking at the purpose and provenance.	Reasons why the source is limited in use – by looking at the purpose and provenance.

Don't worry if you cannot put ideas in all four boxes. It is more important to develop two or three ideas in some detail (for knowledge) and depth of explanation (for source analysis).

Your answer does need to have at least one developed point based on knowledge and one based on source analysis. Ideally, your answer might be set out clearly in two paragraphs to reflect this.

Unit 2 – Sections B and C

There are TWO questions on each of the topics. You have to answer the two questions on ONE topic in Section B and the two questions on ONE topic in Section C.

The pairs of questions on each topic will always be of the same types and in the same order:

- **Explanation – analysis of key features using knowledge; causation; consequence** *8 marks*

  For example, 'Explain the effects of the Wall Street Crash on the people of the USA, 1929–1932.'

When answering this type of question, focus on explanation, not simple description. For the question above you would need to explain, with supporting details, two or more effects to get a high mark.

- **Longer-answer question requiring analysis of an interpretation** *12 marks*

  The question will provide a quotation and ask you the extent to which you agree with the interpretation.

  For example, '"The New Deal did little to help the economic recovery of the USA in the 1930s." How far do you agree with this interpretation? Explain your answer.'

The important thing to concentrate on is ANALYSIS – that is, explaining the reasons why you agree and disagree. The quotation will have been chosen to allow you to do both – that is, partly agree and partly disagree. However, do not expect that there will always be the same balance between them! History is not like that!

For each point you make, try to provide a clear explanation in relation to the quotation, and include relevant factual details. This will mean that you have made a developed point. You need to aim for at least one agreeing point, and one disagreeing point, to get a good mark.

In addition, to get a very high mark, you need to include a clear judgement in relation to the interpretation. Sometimes the judgement might provide an oportunity for differentiation – for example, in the question above, the answer might vary for different years in the 1930s; and for different aspects of the economy – some recovered more than others.

Online resources

This revision guide is also supported by representative example answers to every kind of Exam practice question from all of the chapters – covering both core and depth content – which are available online at www.hodderplus.co.uk/modernworldhistory

- Along with the example answers, a Comment is also given. Reading through these against your answers will help you to build your confidence, improve your answers and, ultimately, your grades.

- Quick quizzes are also available online at www.hodderplus.co.uk/modernworldhistory to test your knowledge of the key content. These accompany the Key content boxes found at the end of each chapter, which allow you to tick off each area as you learn them.

The period 1890–1914 saw rivalry between the Great Powers of Europe, with crises in Morocco and Bosnia bringing war closer. The assassination of the Archduke Franz Ferdinand in July 1914 set off a chain of events that led to the outbreak of the First World War.

Key issues

As with all examination topics, you will be expected to do more than simply learn the content and write it out again. You will need to show understanding of key issues from the period. These are:

- Why were there two armed camps in Europe in 1914?
- Why did war break out in 1914?

1.1 Why were there two armed camps in Europe in 1914?

By 1907, Europe was divided into two rival groups. These were the Triple Alliance of Germany, Austria–Hungary and Italy, and the Triple Entente of Britain, France and Russia.

Development of the Triple Alliance and Triple Entente

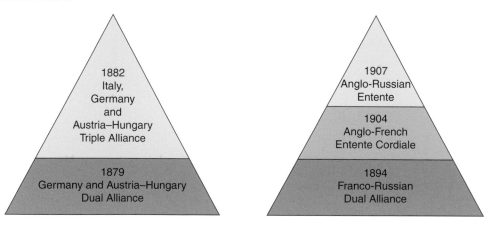

The formation of the Triple Alliance and the Triple Entente.

The Triple Alliance

This alliance was eventually signed in 1882.

- In 1879, the German **Chancellor** Bismarck signed the Dual Alliance with Austria to strengthen Germany against France and Russia.
- Three years later, Italy joined and it became the Triple Alliance. This was a defensive alliance with all three powers agreeing to support each other if one of them was attacked by two or more powers.

> **Exam tip** Be aware of what was agreed in this alliance. This detail will impress an examiner.

> **Key term**
>
> **Chancellor:** chief minister (equivalent of Prime Minister in Britain).

The Triple Entente

This came together in three different stages.

1. The Franco-Russian Dual Alliance of 1894

These two countries allied for several reasons:

- Kaiser Wilhelm II had made it clear that he did not favour close relations with Russia.
- Both France and Russia felt isolated in Europe.
- France was still determined to get revenge on Germany for the defeat of 1871 and wanted to recover the provinces of Alsace–Lorraine.
- Russia was in need of a loan to help develop her economy.

The alliance was defensive, with both countries agreeing to support each other if attacked by Germany or Austria–Hungary.

2. The Entente Cordiale of 1904

At the end of the nineteenth century, Britain played very little part in events in Europe. This isolation, because it was a deliberate British policy, became known as 'splendid isolation'. However, France and Britain, who had been great rivals for many years, surprisingly signed an **entente** in 1904, which became known as the Entente Cordiale. There were several reasons for this:

- Britain felt increasingly isolated, especially as Germany had declined to sign an agreement in the years 1900–02 limiting naval expansion.
- There was increasing rivalry between Germany and Britain due to German naval expansion.
- France continued to want revenge on Germany and the recovery of the lost provinces.
- Britain wanted to stop French interference in Egypt and the French wanted a free hand to expand into Morocco.

> **Key term**
>
> **Entente:** not an alliance, but an agreement to settle differences.

As a result of the Entente Cordiale, France allowed Britain to go ahead with reforms in Egypt, and Britain promised not to oppose any French action in Morocco. Although only a loose agreement, it had several important effects:

- Kaiser Wilhelm was suspicious of the agreement and became determined to break it up.
- It encouraged French expansion in Morocco.
- Anglo-French relations became closer in the years after 1904 so that by 1914 the two countries even planned how to fight a future war against Germany.

3. The Anglo-Russian Entente of 1907

This was signed mainly due to French influence as France was already in alliance with Russia and had signed the Entente Cordiale with Britain. Moreover, Britain and Russia were keen to settle areas of difference in the Middle East, especially Persia, and the Far East. Britain now had agreements with France and Russia and this is often referred to as the Triple Entente, although no such alliance actually existed.

The alliance system, including the Triple Alliance and the Triple Entente, was important because:

- it increased tension in Europe. It was like having two rival gangs fighting for influence
- a dispute between one of the members could well involve the other members. This would turn a dispute between two countries into a major conflict between all six.

Revision tasks

1 Using the information on pages 8–9, complete a copy of the following grid and complete each section.

Alliance/ agreement	Members	Why signed	What agreed
Triple Alliance			
Entente Cordiale			
Anglo-Russian Entente			

2 What is the difference between an alliance and an entente?

3 In five words or fewer, summarise the importance of the alliance system.

Exam tip: q3 You may be asked to describe the key features of the alliance system. You should include references to the Triple Alliance and the Triple Entente, and their effects on international relations.

Kaiser Wilhelm II's aims in foreign policy

Wilhelm became Kaiser (Emperor) of Germany in 1888. His subsequent actions did much to increase tension and rivalry between the Great Powers.

Britain
Wilhelm's actions did much to create rivalry with Britain.

- He was determined to expand the German empire and find a 'place in the sun'. This policy of **Weltpolitik** threatened British interests in the Turkish Empire, Africa and the Far East.

- He was determined to build up a German navy. This threatened British naval supremacy.

France
The Kaiser was determined to challenge the Entente Cordiale by interfering with French interests in Morocco.

Russia
Wilhelm II fully supported the interests of Austria–Hungary in the Balkans. This infuriated Russia.

Key term

Weltpolitik: world policy.

The Moroccan crises of 1905 and 1911 and their effects on the alliances

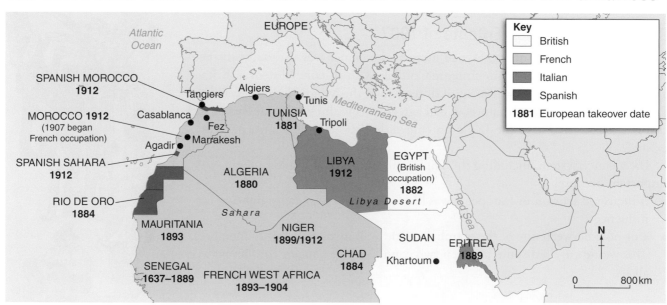

Map showing the Moroccan crises.

These two crises did much to increase rivalry between Britain and Germany and France and Germany.

The first crisis, 1905–06

France already had an empire in North Africa, which included Algeria and Tunisia. Morocco would complete this North African Empire. The Kaiser, however, decided to interfere in Morocco.

- He wanted to test the strength of the Entente Cordiale and hoped to split it apart. He did not believe Britain would stand by France over Morocco.
- He did not want to see France extend her North African Empire.

In 1905, the Kaiser paid a visit to the Moroccan port of Tangiers where he made a speech declaring that Morocco should remain independent of France. This sparked a crisis. France, supported by Britain, refused to back down. However, the French did agree to the Kaiser's demand for an international conference to discuss the future of Morocco.

The conference took place at Algeciras in Spain in 1906 and was a disaster for the Kaiser. Only Austria–Hungary supported his demands for Moroccan independence. Britain fully supported the French. The crisis had important effects on the alliances:

- France was in effect given a free hand in Morocco and was grateful to Britain.
- The Kaiser's attempts to break up the Entente Cordiale had backfired. His interference had strengthened relations between Britain and France.
- Anglo-German rivalry intensified as the Kaiser blamed the British for his humiliating defeat.

The second Moroccan (or Agadir) crisis, 1911

In 1911, the French finally occupied Fez in Morocco. The Kaiser sent a gunboat called the *Panther* to the Moroccan port of Agadir in order to force the French to agree to compensation in the form of the French Congo in central Africa.

However, Germany's actions backfired. Britain was determined to support France as both countries believed that Wilhelm was trying to set up a German naval base in Morocco. Lloyd George, the British Chancellor of the Exchequer and a well-known pacifist, made a speech at Mansion House in London in which he directly warned the Germans that Britain would back the French, by war if necessary. Britain's fleet was even prepared for war. In the end, Germany backed down rather than risk war.

The crisis had several important effects:

- It greatly increased tension in Europe.
- It strengthened the Anglo-French Entente due to British support for the French.
- The Kaiser had suffered another humiliating defeat and was unlikely to back down a third time.
- It increased Anglo-German rivalry. The Kaiser once again blamed his humiliation on the British.

> ### Revision task
>
> Copy and complete the following table to show similarities and differences between the two Moroccan crises.
>
> | | Similarities | Differences |
> | --- | --- | --- |
> | First crisis, 1905–06 | | |
> | Agadir crisis, 1911 | | |

Exam tip Candidates often confuse the key features of these two Moroccan crises. Ensure you revise them thoroughly. You may well be asked to describe the key features of one or both.

Exam practice

1 Which of the two Moroccan crises was the bigger threat to peace in the years 1900–14? Give reasons for your choice.

You must refer to **both** crises in your answer. *(10 marks)*

Exam tip In Exam practice question 1 above, you are being asked to compare the importance of two different events. Ensure you explain each one in your answer. Remember to make a final judgement on the relative importance of each reason for each crisis.

Bosnian crisis 1908–09 and its effects on the alliances

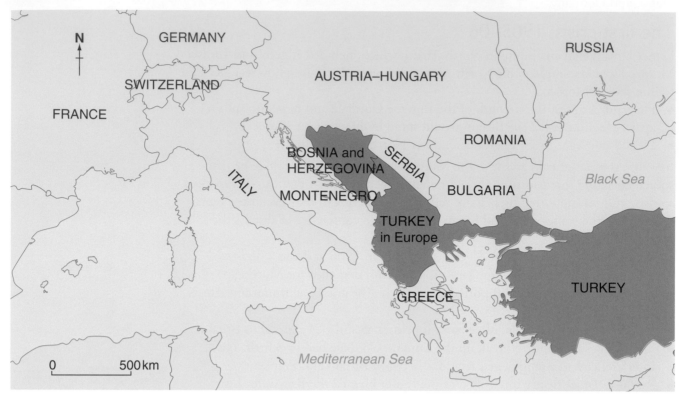

The Balkans in 1908 (shown by the area in red).

In 1908, Austria–Hungary **annexed** Bosnia and Herzegovina. This led to a serious international crisis. The Serbians were furious because they had hoped to make Bosnia part of a greater Serbian state. They appealed to Russia for help. Russia's answer was to call for an international conference to discuss the annexation. Austria–Hungary refused to attend and was fully backed by Germany.

Germany demanded that Russia accept the annexation. Russia had little choice but to back down as its army was no match for German forces. This crisis again increased tension between the Great Powers for several reasons:

- Serbia was furious with Austria–Hungary. It wanted revenge and the return of Bosnia.
- Russia was humiliated but was now unlikely to back down in another crisis.
- Germany was now fully committed to supporting Austro-Hungarian policy in the Balkans, even if it led to war.
- Russia drew even closer to Britain and France.

> ## Key term
>
> **Annexed:** when territory is seized and made part of another country's empire.

> ## Comment
>
> *The Bosnian crisis is often described as a dress rehearsal for the crisis that followed the assassination at Sarajevo in 1914.*

Revision tasks

1 Why did the Bosnian crisis increase rivalry between:
- Austria and Serbia
- Austria and Russia
- Russia and Germany?

2 Why was the crisis settled without resort to war?

The arms race – military and naval

In the years before 1914, there was competition between the Great Powers with regard to the size and strength of their armed forces, including their armies and navies. This arms race encouraged rivalry between the Great Powers as each tried to enlarge and strengthen their armed forces.

Military

Every major power in Europe, except Britain, had introduced **conscription**, which led to huge armies. These armies could be **mobilised** at a moment's notice. In the years 1900–14, the main European powers more than doubled their spending on their armies. Guns, shells, bullets and other weapons were stockpiled in case of war. Even more destructive weapons were developed, such as the machine gun and huge field guns. The arms race brought war nearer because:

- it increased tension between the Great Powers because as one power increased its army, another would follow suit
- it made war more likely – as each country increased its army and weapons it became even more confident of success in a future war and more willing to test its armed forces.

Key terms

Conscription: all males of a certain age group have to serve in the armed forces, usually for one or two years.
Mobilise: to get armed forces ready for battle.

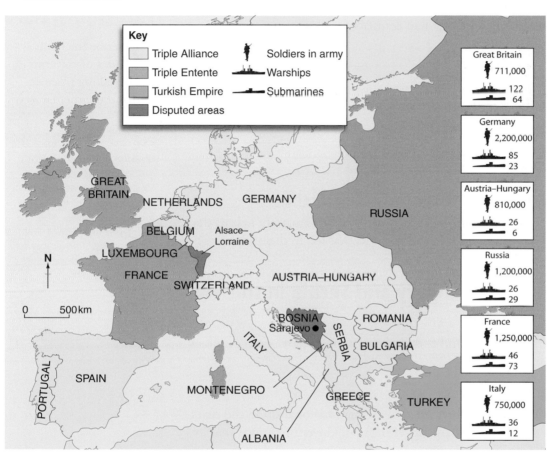

The military capacity of Europe's alliances, 1914.

Naval

Another aspect of the arms race was the naval competition between Britain and Germany in the years 1900–14. The navy was vital to Britain in order to protect its empire, prevent invasion and guarantee its position as a great power. Germany already had the world's best army. However, in 1898, Germany began to build a fleet of battleships to rival the British navy.

At first, this was not a major threat to Britain because the Royal Navy was far superior and it would take Germany many years to catch up. However, this all changed with the launch of the British super-battleship HMS *Dreadnought* in 1906. *Dreadnought* was faster, bigger and had a much greater firing range than existing battleships. It made all previous battleships **obsolete**. This meant that Britain was now only one new battleship ahead of Germany. A race developed between the two countries to see who could build the most. In 1909, Britain had eight Dreadnought battleships to Germany's seven.

Key term

Obsolete: out of date. The old battleships were no match in size, speed or firepower for the Dreadnought. HMS *Dreadnought* represented such a marked advance in naval technology that the name became associated with an entire generation of battleships, known as 'Dreadnoughts'.

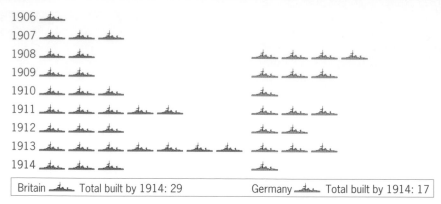

1906		
1907		
1908		
1909		
1910		
1911		
1912		
1913		
1914		

| Britain Total built by 1914: 29 | Germany Total built by 1914: 17 |

Number of Dreadnoughts built by Britain and Germany, 1906–14.

The naval race poisoned relations between Britain and Germany. Britain feared German world domination if the Kaiser had control of both the strongest army and navy.

Revision task

Write your own definitions of the following terms:
- conscription
- Dreadnought
- naval race.

1.2 Why did war break out in 1914?

The assassination in 1914 of Archduke Franz Ferdinand, the Austrian heir to the throne, by a Serbian terrorist set off a chain of events that led to the outbreak of the First World War.

The aims of Austria–Hungary and Serbia in the Balkans

Rivalry between Austria–Hungary and Serbia played a major part in the outbreak of the First World War.

Austria–Hungary

Austria–Hungary felt increasingly threatened by Serbian nationalism in the years after 1900. The main concern of the Austro-Hungarian Government was that the population of Serbs within its empire would want to be part of a greater Serbia, which might in turn lead to a break-up of the Austro-Hungarian Empire. Austria–Hungary, fully supported by Germany, became determined to crush Serbia, especially when it was greatly strengthened by the Balkan Wars of 1912–13.

Serbia

Serbia wished to unite all Serbs living in south-east Europe into an enlarged state of Greater Serbia and was supported by Russia who regarded herself as the protector of all **Slavs**.

The assassination at Sarajevo

On 28 June 1914, Archduke Franz Ferdinand and his wife Sophie were assassinated by Gavrilo Princip, a member of the Black Hand terrorist organisation, during a state visit to Sarajevo. Austria–Hungary was furious and blamed the Serbs. Having secured full backing from the Kaiser, on 23 July Austria–Hungary sent an **ultimatum** to Serbia, which it knew the Serbs would reject.

Comment

Some historians believe that the arms race made war less likely. They argue that the build-up of armies, navies and weapons acted as a deterrent in a similar way to the nuclear arms race that followed the Second World War.

Exam practice

1 Describe the main features of the arms race taking place at this time. *(4 marks)*

Exam tip Exam practice question 1 above is a Unit 1 question. You will need to include precise details of the competition for bigger armies and navies. You will also need to describe two key features. Remember key features can include causes, events or results.

Key terms

Slavs: the name given to the different national groups who live in the Balkans, the area of south-eastern Europe.
Ultimatum: a final demand – or else!

The ultimatum included ten demands that meant the virtual end of Serbian independence. Surprisingly, the Serbs accepted all but one. However, Austria–Hungary, determined on revenge, declared war on Serbia on 28 July 1914.

Revision tasks

1 Summarise in no more than five words the reasons for the rivalry between Austria–Hungary and Serbia.

2 Why did this rivalry involve other great powers?

The events leading to war – the role of alliances in 1914

Each country had to mobilise quickly to gain an advantage. Once one country began to move its troops to the front line, the enemy had to do the same or risk immediate defeat. In other words, once mobilisation began it was difficult to stop. Here are the events that led to the outbreak of the First World War.

28 July	Austria declares war on Serbia.
30 July 	Russia moves its armed forces to help Serbia defend itself against Austria–Hungary. Germany warns Russia to stop mobilising. Russia ignores the warning.
1 August	Germany declares war on Russia and warns France to remain neutral. Italy declares that it will remain neutral.
2 August	France begins to mobilise its armed forces.
3 August	Germany declares war on France.
4 August 	Germany invades Belgium as part of the Schlieffen Plan. Later that day, Britain declares war on Germany.

The Schlieffen Plan and its effects on the outbreak of war

Although the assassination at Sarajevo sparked off a chain of events that led to the outbreak of the First World War, the German invasion of Belgium on 4 August 1914 was due to the Schlieffen Plan.

The Schlieffen Plan

Because of the alliance system, Germany believed it might have to fight a war on two fronts – against France in the west and Russia in the east. As early as 1904, the head of the German army, von Schlieffen, devised a plan to overcome the problem of fighting a war on two fronts:

- The German army was to sweep through Belgium and defeat France in the first few weeks of war.
- This would then allow the German army to move to the Eastern Front to defeat the Russians.

Comment

In 1911, the Black Hand terrorist society formed, which aimed to unite all Serbs into a Greater Serbia. By 1914, it had 2,500 members. It planned to assassinate Archduke Franz Ferdinand, the heir to the throne of Austria–Hungary, when he visited Sarajevo in June 1914.

Comment

It has been suggested that Austria–Hungary deliberately set up the assassination to provide an excuse to crush Serbia. After all, the Archduke travelled in an open-top car and the visit coincided with Serbian National Day.

Exam tip Ensure you know the key dates from 28 June to 4 August 1914. Precise knowledge of dates will impress an examiner.

Comment

It has been suggested that the Schlieffen Plan forced the Germans into a war against France and Russia as it was based on a war on two fronts. This may account for the German declarations of war on Russia and France.

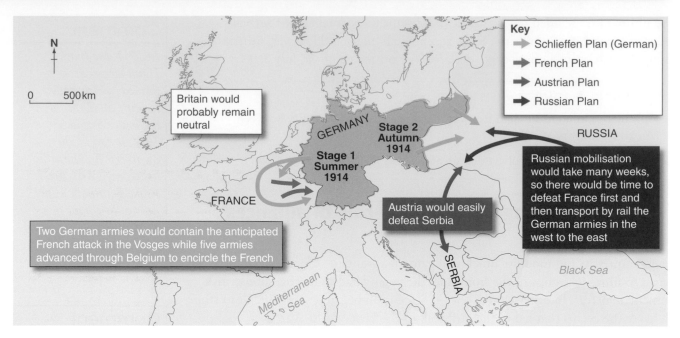

The Schlieffen Plan.

The Schlieffen Plan's effect on the outbreak of war

The German invasion of Belgium on 4 August 1914 brought Britain into the war. The British had no intention of supporting Russia and it would have been difficult for the British Government to convince the British public to go to war simply due to close relations with France. The German invasion of Belgium provided ideal reasons for intervention:

- Belgian neutrality had been guaranteed by the Great Powers, including Prussia, in the 1839 Treaty of London, which the Kaiser described as a 'scrap of paper'.
- The British people were shocked by German aggression against a small nation.

> **Comment**
>
> *In 1871, Prussia became part of a united Germany.*

Responsibility for the outbreak of war

No one country was fully responsible for the outbreak of war in 1914.

Country	Responsibility
France	The French were determined to get revenge on Germany, regaining the lost provinces of Alsace–Lorraine and expanding into Morocco.
Russia	The Tsar fully supported Serbia and its attempts to create a Greater Serbia. Russia began mobilising on 30 July 1914.
Britain	The British took part in the naval race against Germany, supported France during the Moroccan crises, and declared war on Germany after its invasion of Belgium.
Germany	Wilhelm II followed a policy of *Weltpolitik*, threatened Britain with the build up of his navy, challenged France during the Moroccan crises, and fully backed Austria–Hungary in 1908–09 and 1914.
Austria–Hungary	The Austro-Hungarian Government was determined to crush Serbia. It annexed Bosnia in 1908 and declared war on Serbia in July 1914 following Serbia's acceptance of nine of the ten points of the ultimatum.
Serbia	Serbia was determined to create a Greater Serbia that threatened the Austro-Hungarian Empire. It challenged the Austro-Hungarian annexation of Bosnia in 1908. The Black Hand organisation was set up in Serbia and assassinated Franz Ferdinand.

Revision tasks

1 Using a story board or cartoon strip describe the Schlieffen Plan.

2 Give each country responsible for the outbreak of the war a rating of 1–5, with 5 meaning greatest responsibility. Give reasons for your decisions.

3 Draw a timeline to show the main developments of 1890–1914. Indicate on your timeline how these developments increased rivalry between the Great Powers.

4 On one side of A3 paper, summarise the main reasons for increased rivalry and the outbreak of war in 1914.
   - Arrange the reasons clockwise in rank order, beginning with the most important at twelve o'clock.
   - Draw lines to show links between the reasons. Write explanations for these links along the lines.

Key content

You need to have a good working knowledge of the following areas.
Tick off each item once you are confident in your knowledge.

❑ The development and members of the Triple Alliance, the Entente Cordiale and the Anglo-Russian Agreement; Britain's emergence from 'splendid isolation'

❑ Kaiser Wilhelm II's aims in foreign policy: *Weltpolitik*, a 'place in the sun', his attitudes towards Britain and the development of the navy

❑ The Moroccan crises of 1905 and 1911 and their effects on the alliances

❑ The Bosnian crisis of 1908–09 and its effects on the alliances

❑ The arms race – military and naval: why countries increased the size of their armies; the Anglo-German naval race

❑ The aims of Austria–Hungary and Serbia in the Balkans; the role of the Black Hand terrorist group

❑ The assassination at Sarajevo; the response of Austria–Hungary; the ultimatum and Serbia's response

❑ The events leading to the war; the role of the alliances in 1914

❑ The Schlieffen Plan and its effects on the outbreak of war

❑ Responsibility for the outbreak of war

Check your knowledge online with our Quick quizzes at www.hodderplus.co.uk/modernworldhistory.

SOURCE 1

From the *Sunday Times*, 2 August 1914.

Britain has no written alliances with France. But it has an obligation to honour. We have a vital interest in seeing that France is not overwhelmed by Germany.

Exam practice

1 **Source 1** suggests reasons why Britain went to war in August 1914. Do you agree that these were the main reasons? Explain your answer by referring to:
   - the purpose of the source – what is it trying to make you believe?
   - its content – what is it suggesting about British reasons?
   - your own contextual knowledge – in other words, what do you know about the reasons for Britain going to war in 1914? *(6 marks)*

2 Which do you think was the more important reason for the outbreak of the First World War?
   - The murder at Sarajevo
   - The Schlieffen Plan.
   You must refer to **both** reasons in your answer. *(10 marks)*

Exam tip: q2 This is a Unit 1 question. Remember you have to refer to both reasons. Remember to make a final judgement on the relative importance of each reason.

Chapter 2: Peacemaking 1918–1919 and the League of Nations

The First World War was a disaster for Europe. Millions were killed and whole countries were devastated. The victorious leaders met in Paris in 1918 to try to work out how to stop a terrible war like this ever happening again.

Key issues

As with all examination topics, you will be expected to do more than simply learn the content and write it out again. You will need to show understanding of key issues from the period. These are:

- How did the Treaty of Versailles establish peace?
- Why did the League of Nations fail in its attempts to keep peace?

2.1 How did the Treaty of Versailles establish peace?

In November 1918, Germany signed the **armistice** that ended the First World War.

The Paris Peace Conference and the aims of the 'Big Three'

The armistice was followed by the Paris Peace Conference where a peace treaty would be discussed. This was dominated by the 'Big Three' – the leaders of the USA, Britain and France – who had conflicting views about what the peace treaty should do.

The Fourteen Points

In January 1918, President Wilson of the USA had proposed the Fourteen Points, which he said should be the key to a fair peace. His ideas included:

- a ban on secret treaties and a reduction in arms
- the idea that countries should not claim colonies without consulting each other and the local inhabitants
- **self-determination** for countries that were once part of the Turkish and Austro-Hungarian Empires
- independence for Belgium
- France to regain Alsace–Lorraine
- Poland to become an independent state with access to the sea
- a League of Nations to be set up to settle disputes between countries by peaceful means.

Exam tip You do not need to know all Fourteen Points, only the main ideas that are summarised here.

Aims of the Big Three

Leader	Views on peace treaty
Georges Clemenceau of France	During the war, France had suffered enormous damage with large areas of land devastated, many factories destroyed and over 1 million deaths. Clemenceau was under pressure from the French people to make Germany suffer. He also wanted to prevent future threats of a German invasion. Therefore, he wanted a harsh treaty that would punish Germany and cripple its economy so it could not threaten France again.
Woodrow Wilson of the USA	The USA had only been in the war since April 1917. Its war damage and casualties were low compared to France and Britain. Wilson's ideas were very much influenced by the Fourteen Points. Although he believed that Germany was responsible for the war, he did not want to impose a harsh treaty as this would lead to a German desire for revenge and another war. Wilson had two main aims: ● self-determination ● international co-operation – settling disputes by all countries working together.
David Lloyd George of Great Britain	The British people were bitter towards Germany. They wanted a harsh peace treaty and Lloyd George had promised that he would make Germany pay. However, like Wilson, he feared that a harsh treaty might lead to a German desire for revenge and possibly another war. He also wanted Britain and Germany to begin trading with each other again. Lloyd George was often in the middle ground between Clemenceau, who he thought was too extreme, and Wilson, who he believed was too reliant on the Fourteen Points.

Revision tasks

1 What is meant by:
   ● an armistice ● the Fourteen Points ● self-determination?

2 Make a copy of this triangle.
   ● On one side of each line write, in green, any similarities in the aims of each leader.
   ● On the other side, in red, write any differences.

3 Where would you put each leader on this line?

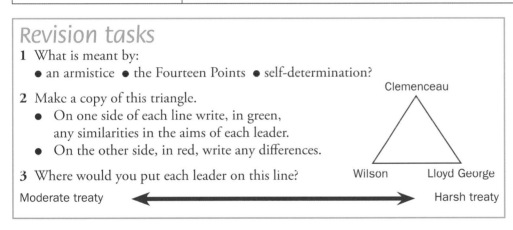

Moderate treaty ⟵⟶ Harsh treaty

Exam practice

1 Describe how the aims of the Big Three differed. *(4 marks)*

Exam tip Exam practice question 1 above is a Unit 1 question. You will need to include precise details of how the aims of the Big Three differed. You will need to describe at least two differences.

The Treaty of Versailles

The treaty was imposed on the German leaders, who were told the terms in May 1919 and forced to sign in the following month. In Germany the peace treaty was called the 'Diktat' because it was dictated rather than negotiated. The main terms were:

War guilt

Article 231, the 'war guilt' clause, said that Germany had to agree that it was responsible for starting the war.

German armed forces

● The army was limited to 100,000.
● Conscription was banned. Soldiers had to be volunteers.
● Germany was not allowed armoured vehicles, submarines or military aircraft.
● The navy could have only six battleships and thirty smaller ships.
● The Rhineland, the area between Germany and France, became a **demilitarised** zone. The Allies were to keep an army of occupation on the west bank of the Rhine for fifteen years. No German troops were allowed into that area.

Key term

Demilitarised: no armed forces or weapons.

Comment

Limiting the size of the German army, and the other military terms, were influenced by Clemenceau to safeguard France against another German invasion.

Reparations

The Allies agreed that Germany had to pay compensation to France, Britain and Belgium for the damage caused by the war. These payments were known as **reparations**. The exact figure of £6,600 million was set by a reparations commission in 1921.

Loss of territories

The Allies agreed that German lands and territories would be rearranged.

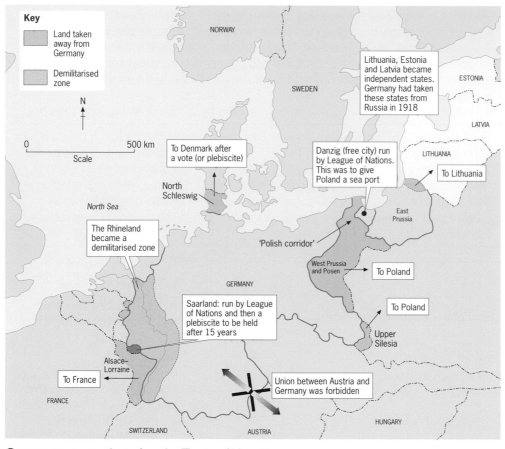

German territories lost after the Treaty of Versailles.

In addition, German colonies, mainly in Africa, were given to France and Britain under the control of the League of Nations.

Anschluss

This means the joining together of Austria and Germany and was forbidden by the Treaty of Versailles.

The League of Nations

Previous methods of keeping the peace had failed and so the League of Nations was set up as an international 'police force' (see pages 22–3). Germany would not be invited to join the League until it could prove it was a peace-loving country.

Comment

The terms of the reparations were influenced by Clemenceau who wanted to cripple the German economy.

Comment

The territorial terms were partly influenced by Clemenceau with the return of Alsace–Lorraine, but also by Wilson and his belief in self-determination in eastern Europe.

Exam tip Candidates are frequently asked questions about the terms of the Treaty of Versailles. The more precise and detailed your knowledge, the higher your marks.

The strengths and weaknesses of the Treaty of Versailles

Strengths	Weaknesses
• The Treaty of Versailles brought peace to Europe and set up an international organisation, the League of Nations, to preserve the peace. • In some ways it was lenient towards Germany which, unlike Austria–Hungary, remained one country with a population of 60 million compared to the 40 million of France. • Germany had imposed a much harsher treaty on Russia, the Treaty of Brest-Litovsk, in March 1918. Russia had lost nearly one-third of its land area.	• It left Germany with a number of grievances. • The Germans could not afford to make the reparations payments. • Britain and France fell out over German reparation payments. • The treaty punished Germany enough to want revenge but not enough to stop her from recovering and seeking revenge. • Wilson pinned too much faith on the League of Nations.

Why Germany objected to the treaty

The Germans reacted to the Treaty of Versailles with horror and outrage.

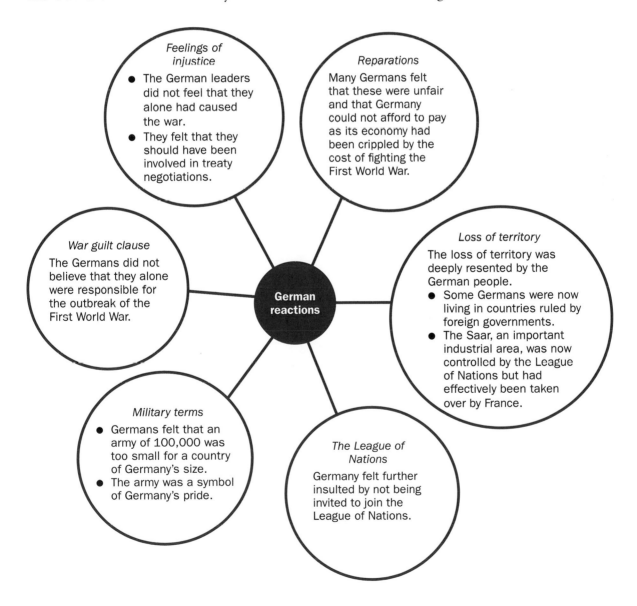

Feelings of injustice
- The German leaders did not feel that they alone had caused the war.
- They felt that they should have been involved in treaty negotiations.

Reparations
Many Germans felt that these were unfair and that Germany could not afford to pay as its economy had been crippled by the cost of fighting the First World War.

War guilt clause
The Germans did not believe that they alone were responsible for the outbreak of the First World War.

German reactions

Loss of territory
The loss of territory was deeply resented by the German people.
- Some Germans were now living in countries ruled by foreign governments.
- The Saar, an important industrial area, was now controlled by the League of Nations but had effectively been taken over by France.

Military terms
- Germans felt that an army of 100,000 was too small for a country of Germany's size.
- The army was a symbol of Germany's pride.

The League of Nations
Germany felt further insulted by not being invited to join the League of Nations.

Revision tasks

Using the information on pages 18–21, answer the following questions.

1 Choose five words to summarise the terms dealing with Germany's armed forces.

2 Explain whether or not you think the reparations bill was too large, and why.

3 Note three examples of territory lost by Germany.

4 Make your own version of the diagram on German reactions (page 21). On your copy, arrange the reasons for German opposition to the Treaty of Versailles clockwise in rank order, beginning with those you think are the most important at twelve o'clock.

5 In your view, which of the Big Three would have been most satisfied with the Treaty of Versailles? Give reasons for your answer.

Exam practice

1 Which was the more important reason for German opposition to the treaty?
  ● Reparations
  ● Military terms
You must refer to **both** reasons in your answer. *(10 marks)*

> **Exam tip** Exam practice question 1 on the left is a Unit 1 question. Remember to mention both factors in your answer. Remember to make a final judgement on the relative importance of each reason.

2.2 Why did the League of Nations fail in its attempts to keep peace?

The League of Nations was set up in 1920.

Membership

When the League was created, there were 42 original member countries. By 1930, membership had increased to nearly 60. However, at any one time, several of the larger and more powerful nations were not members, including:
● the USA, who refused to join
● the defeated nations (including Germany) who, at first, were not allowed to join
● Russia, who was not allowed to join because of its Communist government.

The Covenant of the League

The **Covenant** laid out the aims of the League, which were to:
● prevent aggression by any nation
● encourage co-operation between nations
● work towards international disarmament
● improve the living and working conditions of all peoples.

The League was built upon the idea of collective security. This meant that the members of the League could prevent war by acting together to protect and defend the interests of all nations.

> **Key term**
> **Covenant:** a set of rules.

The organisation of the League

The Assembly

This was the debating chamber of the League and was located at the League's headquarters in Geneva, Switzerland. When the League began there were 42 members, each with a vote in the Assembly that met once a year. It had the powers to admit new members, elect permanent members to the Council and suggest changes to existing peace treaties.

Exam tip Candidates often score low marks on the organisation of the League because they fail to revise this section thoroughly.

Key term

Economic sanctions: restrictions on trade with another country.

The Council

This met up to three times a year and in times of emergency. It had five permanent and four temporary members.
- The five permanent members were the major powers: Britain, France, Italy, Japan and, from 1926, Germany.
- The four temporary members were elected for three years at a time.

The Permanent Court of International Justice

This court was based at the Hague in the Netherlands. It was made up of judges who represented the different legal systems of member countries. It gave decisions on disputes between two countries if asked, but had no way of enforcing its decisions.

The Secretariat

This was the civil service that carried out the work and administration of the League. It kept records of League meetings and prepared reports for the different organisations of the League.

The International Labour Organisation (ILO)

This existed to bring about the League's aim of improving working conditions around the world. Representatives of governments, workers and employers met each year to set minimum standards and persuade members to adopt them.

Commissions

These were set up to carry out specialist work. Some of them existed only for a short period of time, such as the Refugees Commission, which helped First World War refugees return to their homes. Other commissions were more permanent, such as those set up to deal with slavery and health.

Peacekeeping role

The main duty of the Council was to resolve any disputes that might occur between states. It was hoped that this would be done by negotiation. If any country was considered to have started a war through an act of aggression, then such a war became the concern of all the countries in the League who would take action against the aggressor. This action was in three stages:
- **moral condemnation**, which meant that all countries would put pressure on the aggressor in order to make them feel guilty and shame them into stopping the war and accepting the League's decision
- **economic sanctions**, which meant that all countries in the League would stop trading with the aggressor
- **military force**, in which countries in the League would contribute to an armed force that would act against the aggressor.

Exam practice

1 Describe the main features of the organisation of the League. *(4 marks)*

Exam tip Exam practice question 1 above is a Unit 1 question. The more precise your description, the higher your marks. You will need to describe two key features. Remember key features can include causes, events or results.

Revision tasks

1 Produce a key word list of four to six words to summarise the aims of the League of Nations.

2 Give two differences between the Council and the Assembly of the League.

3 What was meant by 'collective security'?

The Manchurian crisis, 1931–33

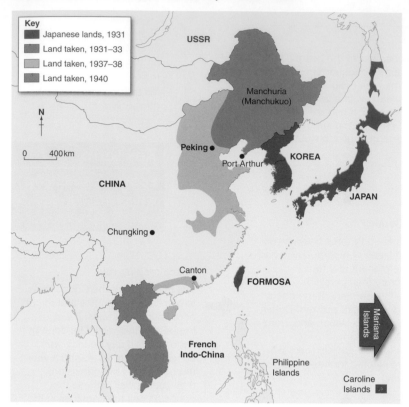

Key
- Japanese lands, 1931
- Land taken, 1931–33
- Land taken, 1937–38
- Land taken, 1940

USSR

Manchuria (Manchukuo)

Peking ●

Port Arthur ●

KOREA

CHINA

Chungking ●

Canton ●

FORMOSA

JAPAN

French Indo-China

Philippine Islands

Mariana Islands

Caroline Islands

N

0   400 km

Japanese expansion, 1931–40.

This crisis was the first major challenge to the League of Nations.

Causes

Japan was a rising power in Asia and the Pacific and had developed very quickly into a modern trading nation in the early twentieth century. However, the Wall Street Crash had a major impact on the Japanese economy. **Protectionist** policies in the USA and other countries led to a loss of trade. Japan looked for other ways to expand.

In 1931, the Japanese used the excuse of an attack by Chinese troops on a Japanese railway to invade the Chinese territory of Manchuria. Manchuria was rich in natural resources and raw materials and provided a market for Japanese goods. The invasion was a success and Manchuria was renamed Manchukuo.

Events

China was in the middle of a civil war and was unable to defend Manchuria. The Chinese appealed to the League for support against the Japanese. The League sent a commission, the Lytton Commission, to investigate the crisis. The commission was very slow and took over a year to investigate, by which time the invasion and occupation had been completed.

The League accepted the findings of the report, condemned the actions of the Japanese, and asked the Japanese to withdraw from the province. The Japanese left the League and remained in control of Manchuria.

Results

This event marked the beginning of the end for the League.
- Britain and France were not willing to support the League in taking action against the Japanese.
- The League had failed to prevent aggression. This encouraged later aggression by Italy and Germany.

> **Exam tip** You will often be asked how and why the Manchurian crisis contributed to the failure of the League of Nations. In other words, why were events in Manchuria important for the League as a whole?

> **Key term**
>
> **Protectionist:** the economic theory of using the tax system to protect home industries in the face of foreign competition.

> **Comment**
>
> *Britain and France both had empires in the Far East and feared possible further Japanese aggression if they fully supported the League.*

The Abyssinian crisis

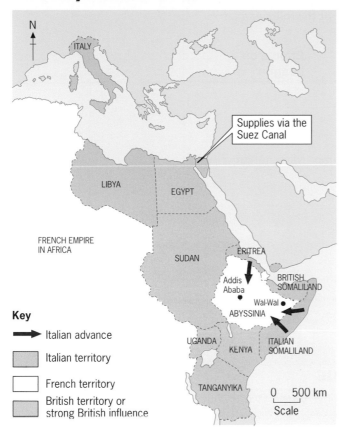

Italian expansion, 1935–36.

Causes

In 1935, Italian troops invaded the African country of Abyssinia.

- Mussolini had ruled Italy since 1922 and wanted to increase Italy's prestige as a world power by increasing its territories in Africa.
- Abyssinia was one of the few countries in Africa not under European control.
- The Italians wanted revenge for a humiliating defeat by the Abyssinians at the Battle of Adowa, 1896.

Events

The Emperor of Abyssinia, Haile Selassie, appealed to the League for assistance. The League condemned Italian aggression and imposed economic sanctions against Italy. However, these sanctions did not include oil and Italy continued to trade with non-League members such as the USA. France and Britain did not want to offend Mussolini and drive him closer to Hitler and Germany. The British foreign secretary even worked out a plan with the French, known as the Hoare–Laval Pact, to offer Mussolini most of Abyssinia. However, the plan had to be withdrawn when it was leaked to the public.

Results

The effects of the Abyssinian crisis were serious, resulting in the end of the League as a peacekeeping organisation, as it could no longer be taken seriously.

- The crisis showed that League members were not willing to use force to stop aggression.
- The secret deal, the Hoare–Laval Pact, showed that Britain and France were undermining the League.

Comment

The League remained in existence until the Second World War but became little more than a 'talking shop'.

Revision tasks

1 Using the information on pages 24–25, complete a copy of the following table. Fill in each box in five words or fewer.

	Causes	Events	Effects on League
Manchurian crisis			
Abyssinian crisis			

2 Which of the following were involved with the Abyssinian or Manchurian crises?
- Lytton Commission
- Hoare-Laval Pact
- China
- Haile Selassie
- Mussolini
- Economic sanctions

Put each term in the correct column of the table below.

Manchuria	Abyssinia

Key term

Veto: the right to block a decision made by others.

Reasons for the collapse of the League

- The League lacked key members from the start of the First World War including the defeated nations, Russia, and the USA.
- The League was seen as an exclusive club of victors which was very much dependent on Anglo-French co-operation. However the two countries fell out over the French occupation of the Ruhr in January 1923.
- The organisation of the League made it difficult for it to act quickly because one country could easily **veto** League action.
- The League lacked 'teeth'. Sanctions were often only applied in a half-hearted fashion and the League had no army.
- The world Depression had caused mass unemployment in the early 1930s, as well as a huge drop in trade. Little money or attention was available for world problems that seemed distant, such as the crises in Abyssinia and Manchuria.

Comment

President Wilson founded the League but many Americans did not want the USA involved. They believed their country would be dragged into more European disputes and so supported a policy of isolationism. The League therefore did not have the support of the richest and most powerful country in the world.

Revision tasks

1 Why were the following countries not members of the League in 1920?
- Germany
- Russia
- USA

2 If you were the leader of a small country thinking of joining the League in 1920, what advantages and disadvantages do you think membership would give you? Complete a table like the one below.

Advantages	Disadvantages

3 Make a sketch of a target like the one on the right. Put the reasons for the failure of the League in rank order, beginning with the one you think is the most important in the middle. Explain your decisions.

SOURCE 1

PUNCH, OR THE LONDON CHARIVARI.—AUGUST 14, 1935.

THE AWFUL WARNING.

FRANCE AND ENGLAND (together?).

"WE DON'T WANT YOU TO FIGHT, BUT, BY JINGO, IF YOU DO, WE SHALL PROBABLY ISSUE A JOINT MEMORANDUM SUGGESTING A MILD DISAPPROVAL OF YOU."

A British cartoon of 1935. The figure on the right is Mussolini.

Key content

You need to have a good working knowledge of the following areas.
Tick off each item once you are confident in your knowledge.

❑ The different motives of the Big Three at Versailles
❑ The main terms of the Treaty of Versailles
❑ The strengths and weaknesses of the Treaty of Versailles
❑ The reasons for German opposition to the treaty
❑ The aims, membership and organisation of the League of Nations
❑ The causes, events and results of the Manchurian crisis
❑ The causes, events and results of the Abyssinian crisis
❑ The reasons for the collapse of the League

Check your knowledge online with our Quick quizzes at www.hodderplus.co.uk/modernworldhistory.

Exam practice

1 **Source 1** suggests reasons for the failure of the League in the Abyssinian crisis. Do you agree that these were the main reasons? Explain your answer by referring to:
   - the purpose of the source – what is it trying to make you believe?
   - its content – what is it suggesting about the League?
   - your own contextual knowledge – in other words, what do you know about the failure of the Abyssinian crisis? *(6 marks)*

2 Which was the more important reason for the failure of the League?
   - Membership
   - Lack of power.

   You must refer to **both** reasons in your answer. *(10 marks)*

Exam tip: q2 This is a Unit 1 question. Remember to focus on the question itself, evaluating the importance of each reason in the failure of the League of Nations.

Chapter 3: Hitler's foreign policy and the origins of the Second World War

In January 1933, Adolf Hitler became Chancellor of Germany. By September 1939, the world was at war again. How did this happen?

Key issues

As with all examination topics, you will be expected to do more than simply learn the content and write it out again. You will need to show understanding of key issues from the period. These are:

- How did Hitler challenge and exploit the Treaty of Versailles, January 1933–March 1938?
- Why did Chamberlain's policy of appeasement fail to prevent the outbreak of war in 1939?

3.1 How did Hitler challenge and exploit the Treaty of Versailles, January 1933–March 1938?

Hitler's aims

From January 1933, German foreign policy was controlled by Hitler.

- He immediately took his country out of the League of Nations, which Germany had been allowed to join in 1926.
- Hitler saw the Treaty of Versailles as one of the major causes of Germany's problems. He promised the German people that he would reverse the treaty and retake the territory that Germany had lost.
- In the longer term, he planned to expand into eastern Europe to give the German people *Lebensraum*, which Hitler believed they needed.

Hitler took the following steps to achieve these aims:

- Each time he took over some more territory he managed to convince many European leaders, including Britain's, that once Germany had obtained territory lost at Versailles, no further demands would be made.
- Hitler had the benefit of seeing another country, Japan, successfully defy the League of Nations over Manchuria (see page 24).
- He also eventually developed close relations with Mussolini, who withdrew from the League as a result of the Abyssinian crisis (see page 25).

The return of the Saar

The industrial area of the Saar was taken from Germany by the Treaty of Versailles and put under the control of the League of Nations. A **plebiscite** was to be held among the population after 15 years to decide whether it should be returned to Germany. The plebiscite was held in January 1935, and over 90 per cent voted in favour. Hitler greeted this result as a huge triumph, and declared that this was the first of the injustices of Versailles to be reversed.

Comment

Historians differ in their view of Hitler's foreign policy. Some believe that he planned for war from the beginning. Others see Hitler as an opportunist who took chances when they arose.

Key terms

Lebensraum: living space. Hitler wanted to expand eastwards to create more space for the growing German population.
Plebiscite: a vote by the people of a state or region on an important question, such as union with another country.

Hitler and rearmament

One of Hitler's first steps on coming to power was to increase Germany's armed forces although, at first, he did this secretly due to the terms of the Treaty of Versailles.

The Disarmament Conference, 1932–34

This conference first met in February 1932. The main problem was what to do about Germany. Germany had been in the League for six years. Most people now accepted that the Germans should be treated more equally than the terms of the Treaty of Versailles stipulated. The big question was whether everyone else should disarm to the level that Germany had been forced to, or whether the Germans should be allowed to rearm to the level of the other powers.

Indeed the Germans walked out of the conference in July 1932 when the other powers failed to agree to disarm down to the level of Germany. In May 1933 Hitler returned to the conference and promised not to rearm if 'in five years all other nations destroyed their arms'. When they refused, Hitler withdrew from the conference in October 1933 and, soon after, from the League of Nations.

Non-Aggression Pact with Poland, 1934

In January 1934, Germany signed a non-aggression agreement with Poland. This was signed for several reasons:

- Hitler was hoping to weaken the existing alliance between France and Poland.
- He hoped to reduce Polish fears of German aggression.
- He wanted to show that he had no quarrel with Poland, only with the USSR.

Rearmament

In 1935, Hitler openly staged a massive military rally celebrating the German armed forces. In the same year, he re-introduced conscription and announced a peacetime army of 550,000. A new Air Ministry was to train pilots and build 1,000 aircraft. He was breaking the terms of the Treaty of Versailles, but he guessed correctly that he would get away with rearmament, especially after the collapse of the Disarmament Conference.

Representatives from France, Italy and Britain met in a town called Stresa where they agreed to work together to preserve the peace in Europe. They condemned German rearmament. This became known as the Stresa Front against German aggression, but it did not last long. It collapsed due to the Abyssinian crisis (see page 25), which destroyed close relations between France, Britain and Italy, and the Anglo-German Naval Treaty.

Anglo-German Naval Treaty, 1935

Hitler knew that Britain had some sympathy with Germany on the issue of rearmament. Britain believed that the limits imposed by the Treaty of Versailles were too tight and that a strong Germany was a buffer against Communism. Indeed, in 1935 Britain signed a naval agreement with Germany that allowed the Germans to build their navy up to 35 per cent of the size of the British navy and have the same number of submarines. Britain was accepting Hitler's breach of the Treaty of Versailles.

> **Exam tip** Candidates often have limited knowledge of German rearmament. Ensure you revise the key features of Hitler's policies in the years 1933–35.

Revision tasks

1 What was meant by *Lebensraum*?

2 Explain why Hitler felt so triumphant about the return of the Saar.

3 Give three reasons why Hitler was successful in his policy of rearmament in the years 1933–35.

The remilitarisation of the Rhineland, 1936

Hitler took further steps to reverse the Treaty of Versailles in March 1936 when he began moving German troops back into the Rhineland.

This was a calculated risk for Hitler because:

- the reoccupation of the Rhineland was a clear breach of the Versailles Treaty (see the map on page 20)
- German troops were in no position to stand up to the French army if it reacted (Hitler's troops were under strict orders to retreat if this happened).

The *Anschluss* with Austria, 1938

Hitler had been born in Austria and one of his objectives was to see Germany and Austria united as one country. By 1938, Hitler felt ready to try.

- Hitler bullied the Austrian Chancellor, Schuschnigg, into accepting a Nazi, Seyss-Inquart, as Austrian Minister of the Interior.
- Schuschnigg ordered a plebiscite to be held to find out if the Austrian people really wanted union with Germany.
- Hitler feared a 'no' vote, so he moved German troops to the Austrian border, and threatened to invade if Schuschnigg did not resign in favour of Seyss-Inquart.
- Seyss-Inquart became Chancellor of Austria and invited German troops into the country. On 12 March 1938, the German army entered Vienna. The *Anschluss* was complete.
- The Nazis organised their own vote about union with Germany and, of those who voted, 99 per cent voted in favour. Austria immediately became a province of the new German Reich (empire).

The *Anschluss* with Austria was another clear breach of the Versailles Treaty. The British and French Governments complained about the German violation of the treaty but took no action. Again, there was a feeling among some people in Britain that the treaty had been harsh and Britain should not defend it.

Comment

The reaction to Hitler's remilitarisation of the Rhineland was the beginning of the controversial policy of appeasement. Britain and France certainly did not want war. They felt that they were not strong enough to go to war and were therefore prepared to give Hitler what he wanted.

Key term

Anschluss: union between Austria and Germany.

Revision task

Make a copy of the following grid. Write key words in each part of the table.

	Causes	Events	Results
Remilitarisation of the Rhineland			
The *Anschluss*			

Exam practice

1 Describe how Hitler reoccupied the Rhineland in 1936. *(4 marks)*

2 Which was the bigger threat to European peace in the 1930s?
- German rearmament 1933–35
- The *Anschluss* of 1938

You must refer to **both** threats in your answer. *(10 marks)*

Exam tip: q1 This is a Unit 1 question. Ensure your description is precise.

Exam tip: q2 This is a Unit 1 question. Make sure you refer to both threats in your answer and come to a judgement. You could decide that both threatened peace to the same degree.

3.2 Why did Chamberlain's policy of appeasement fail to prevent the outbreak of war in 1939?

From 1935 to 1938, Britain followed a policy of appeasement – that is, giving in to demands made by Hitler when they were thought to be reasonable. This policy is closely associated with Neville Chamberlain, who was British Prime Minister from 1937 to 1940.

Appeasement

It is easy with the benefit of hindsight to argue that British politicians such as Neville Chamberlain should have done more to prevent German aggression. However, many people in Britain and France at the time agreed with the policy.

Arguments for appeasement	Arguments against appeasement
• Many people remembered the horrors of the First World War and wanted to avoid another war at all costs. • Many people believed that Germany had been treated too harshly under the Treaty of Versailles. • Some people saw Communism as the biggest threat to European stability. They thought that Germany could act as a buffer, especially as Hitler was very anti-Communist. • Britain was not ready for war. Rearmament only started slowly in 1936, and the British forces were no match for the Germans in 1938. • Britain was preoccupied with the problems caused by the Depression, especially high unemployment, and wanted to stay out of unnecessary foreign involvement. • The events of the Spanish Civil War showed how powerful Germany was. Germany's forces had intervened on the side of the Spanish leader, Franco, and what they did showed how horrific another war was likely to be.	• It gave Hitler the advantage. He grew stronger and stronger. When war came it was against a strong Germany. It was fought in Poland, a country too far away for Britain to help. • It was not right. Britain and France allowed Hitler to break international agreements, especially the Treaty of Versailles. The Covenant of the League of Nations had been signed by all its members. They were also prepared to give away parts of other countries, especially Czechoslovakia, to keep the peace. Appeasement was simply another word for weakness and cowardice. • Chamberlain misjudged Hitler. He believed Hitler was a normal leader who would listen to reason. He didn't realise, until it was too late, that appeasement simply encouraged Hitler to believe that he could do anything. • The appeasers missed excellent opportunities to stop Hitler, especially over the reoccupation of the Rhineland in 1936. • The biggest argument against appeasement is it did not stop war coming in 1939.

Exam tip Do not simply criticise appeasement. Be aware of the arguments in favour of appeasement, especially that the majority of British people wanted to avoid another world war.

The Sudeten crisis and Munich Agreement, 1938

Encouraged by his successes, Hitler took his plans a stage further and began to set his sights on Czechoslovakia, a new state set up after the First World War.

The Sudeten crisis

Part of Czechoslovakia consisted of German-speaking peoples in the area known as the Sudetenland. It was this area that next received Hitler's attention.

• Hitler ordered Henlein (the leader of the Sudeten Germans) to stir up trouble in the Sudetenland.

- German newspapers produced allegations of crimes apparently committed by Czechs against Sudeten Germans.
- Hitler threatened war if a solution was not found.

The British Prime Minister, Chamberlain, believed that a peaceful solution could be worked out. He tried to persuade the Czech President, Beneš, to accept self-government for the Sudetenland. Beneš reluctantly agreed, but Hitler then produced new demands in which he claimed the Sudetenland should be part of the German Reich.

On 22 September, at a meeting at Godesberg, Beneš refused to accept the German demands. It seemed that war was a real possibility, but Chamberlain appealed to Hitler to give him more time to find a settlement.

The Munich Agreement

On 29 September, Chamberlain made one last effort to maintain peace.
- He met with Daladier, the French leader, Hitler and Mussolini at Munich in a final bid to resolve the Sudeten crisis.
- Czech representatives were not invited to the meeting.
- The Czechs were forced to hand over the Sudetenland to Germany and a commission was set up to decide precisely which territory the Czechs would lose.

Chamberlain and Hitler had a further meeting in Munich in which both men agreed that Britain and Germany would not go to war. Hitler promised he did not want the rest of Czechoslovakia. Chamberlain returned to Britain a hero, apparently having saved Europe from war.

The results of the Munich Agreement were extremely serious for Czechoslovakia and Europe as a whole.
- The Czech Government was completely humiliated.
- The vital area of the Sudetenland was lost and, in October and November 1938, Hungary and Poland also occupied other parts of Czech territory.
- Britain and France had again given in to Hitler.

Although the Munich Agreement was initially seen as a success, Britain and France increased the pace of their rearmament programmes.

Revision tasks

Using the information on page 31 and above, answer the following questions.

1 Which do you think is the most powerful reason:
- in support of appeasement
- against appeasement?
Explain your choices.

2 Draw a flow chart to show the key features of the Sudeten crisis.

3 Make a copy of the table below. In fewer than five words, explain the consequences of the Munich Agreement for each country.

	Consequences
Britain	
Germany	
Czechoslovakia	

4 The Czechs felt they were betrayed. Do you agree?

Exam practice

1 Describe the main features of the Munich Agreement. *(4 marks)*

Exam tip Exam practice question 1 above is a Unit 1 question. Ensure your description is precise. You will need to describe two key features. Remember key features can include causes, events or results.

The collapse of Czechoslovakia, March 1939

In March 1939, Czechoslovakia finally disappeared from the map of Europe.
- Hitler invaded and occupied what was left of Czechoslovakia.
- Bohemia and Moravia became German protectorates (controlled by Germany).
- Slovakia remained independent in theory, but was dominated by Germany.
- Ruthenia was handed over to Hungary.

The end of appeasement

The final occupation of Czechoslovakia suggested that war was on its way.
- Hitler's promises made at Munich were clearly worthless.
- Britain and France were rapidly rearming and it was accepted that the policy of appeasement had failed.

The Pact of Steel, May 1939

In the spring of 1939, the tide of events seemed to be favouring the dictators.
- In March, Hitler forced the Lithuanians to hand over the Baltic town of Memel and a portion of land along their south-west border.
- In April, General Franco's nationalist forces, supported by Germany and Italy, took power in Spain.
- In May, Mussolini followed Hitler's example in Czechoslovakia by invading Albania.

In May 1939, Hitler and Mussolini signed the Pact of Steel in which they promised to act side by side in future events. Europe was now firmly divided into two camps. Both Britain and France began to look to the USSR as a possible source of support against Germany.

Poland, 1939

Poland was Hitler's next target. Under the Treaty of Versailles, German territory had been handed over to the Poles to give them access to the Baltic Sea (the 'Polish Corridor') and the German city of Danzig had been put under the control of the League of Nations. Following his success in Czechoslovakia, in March 1939 Hitler demanded the return of Danzig and the Polish Corridor.

The French and British Governments, humiliated by Munich and the events that followed, now acted decisively.
- In April, they gave guarantees of support against German aggression to the Polish, Greek and Romanian Governments.
- They increased production of arms and equipment.

The role of the USSR, 1938–39, and the Nazi-Soviet Pact

In April 1939, Britain and France had guaranteed the frontiers of Poland against any attack. In fact, there was no way that they could help Poland if it had been attacked because of its distance from the west. The only country that could defend Poland against any German attack was the USSR. Britain and France began talks with the USSR to try to reach an agreement.

The role of the USSR, 1938–39

Throughout the 1930s, the Soviets felt that Britain had been trying to direct Hitler to the east, and it is true that there were many in Britain who feared communism more than fascism. Evidence of this was the USSR's exclusion from the Munich Conference when clearly the future of Czechoslovakia was important to them. In 1939, Britain and France showed no urgency in making an agreement with the

USSR. This made Stalin, the Soviet leader, more suspicious of their aims and led to him signing the Nazi-Soviet Pact with Hitler in August 1939.

The Nazi-Soviet Pact

On 23 August 1939, the German Foreign Minister, Ribbentrop, and Soviet Foreign Minister, Molotov, signed the Nazi-Soviet Non-Aggression Pact.

- The Soviets and Germans agreed not to fight each other in the event of war in Europe.
- Both powers secretly agreed to divide up Polish territory should war occur.
- Hitler gave Stalin a free hand to occupy part of Romania and the Baltic states of Latvia, Estonia and Lithuania.

The news of the Nazi-Soviet Pact stunned the world because Hitler and Stalin represented two totally opposing political systems (Nazism and Communism). However, on closer inspection, the Nazi-Soviet Pact comes as less of a surprise. Despite their different political beliefs, Hitler and Stalin had much to offer each other.

- For Hitler, the pact removed the threat of war on two fronts. It also gave him the opportunity he needed to deal with Poland, despite the threats coming from Britain and France.
- Stalin had been suspicious of the British and French approaches – before the rise of Hitler they had shown little friendship to the USSR. Hitler, however, had more to offer the Soviets (for example, territory in eastern Europe).

Poland and the outbreak of war

Soon after the signing of the Nazi-Soviet Non-Aggression Pact, Hitler decided to invade Poland. What gave him the confidence to go ahead?

- The Pact allowed him to deal with the Polish problem without having to worry about a possible Soviet attack.
- The British and French guarantees of support for Poland in April 1939 were too late to convince him that they really were willing to go to war.
- The policy of appeasement had given him the impression that the British and French Governments would agree to almost anything in order to prevent another war with Germany.
- Even if war was declared, Poland was too far away for Britain and France to provide practical support. If war came, Hitler decided, it would be over very quickly and he would have achieved another of his objectives.

On 1 September 1939, German troops invaded Poland. Britain and France declared war soon after. On 15 September, the USSR also invaded Poland and took the territory agreed in the Nazi-Soviet Pact. Within six weeks, Poland had been defeated and, like Czechoslovakia, disappeared from the map of Europe.

> **Exam tip** The events of March–September 1939 are complex. Ensure you have a clear understanding of the sequence of events that led to war.

Responsibility for the outbreak of war

Although Hitler is blamed for the outbreak of war, other countries must also bear some responsibility:

- **Germany**: Hitler made impossible demands on Poland and eventually invaded on 1 September 1939.
- **USSR**: Stalin made a deal with Hitler that cleared the way for a German invasion.
- **Poland**: signed an alliance with Britain and France that encouraged it to resist German demands.
- **Britain and France**: their policy of appeasement made Hitler believe they would not resist his invasion of Poland. Their guarantees to Poland encouraged Poland to refuse Hitler's demands.

Revision task

Create a timeline with key details of each event from 1935–39 like the one below.

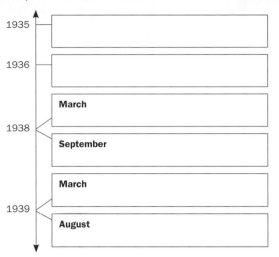

Exam practice

1 Which was a more important reason for the outbreak of war in September 1939?
- the collapse of Czechoslovakia, March 1939
- the Nazi-Soviet Pact, August 1939

You must refer to **both** reasons in your answer. *(10 marks)*

SOURCE 1

From the *Daily Express*, 30 September 1938.

People of Britain, your children are safe. Your husbands and sons will not march to war. Peace is a victory for all mankind. If we must have a victor, let us choose Chamberlain, for the Prime Minister's conquests are mighty and enduring – millions of happy homes and hearts relieved of their burdens.

2 **Source 1** shows one reaction to the Munich Agreement. Do you agree that this was the main reaction? Explain your answer by referring to:
- the purpose of the source – what is it trying to make you believe?
- its content – what is it suggesting are the immediate reactions to the Agreement?
- your own contextual knowledge – in other words, what do you know about the reactions to the Agreement? *(6 marks)*

Exam tip: q1 Exam practice question 1 on the left is a Unit 1 question. Ensure you refer to both reasons in your answer and come to a judgement. You could decide that both reasons were of equal importance.

Key content

You need to have a good working knowledge of the following areas.
Tick off each item once you are confident in your knowledge.

- ❏ Hitler's aims in foreign policy
- ❏ The return of the Saar
- ❏ Hitler's policy of rearmament in the years 1933–35
- ❏ The reoccupation of the Rhineland
- ❏ The *Anschluss* with Austria, March 1938
- ❏ The Sudeten crisis
- ❏ The Munich Agreement
- ❏ The collapse of Czechoslovakia
- ❏ The Nazi-Soviet Pact of August 1939
- ❏ The German invasion of Poland and the outbreak of war

Check your knowledge online with our Quick quizzes at www.hodderplus.co.uk/modernworldhistory.

Chapter 4: The origins of the Cold War, 1945–1960

During the Second World War, the USA and the USSR had fought together as allies against Germany and Japan. Once this war was won, relations between the two 'superpowers' quickly deteriorated. A new war began – a war of ideas – and so it was known as the Cold War.

Key issues

As with all examination topics, you will be expected to do more than simply learn the content and write it out again. You will need to show understanding of key issues from the period. These are:

- Why did the USA and the USSR become rivals in the years 1945–49?
- How did the Cold War develop in the years 1949–60?

4.1 Why did the USA and the USSR become rivals in the years 1945–49?

Rivalry between the USA and USSR was due to ideological differences between the two superpowers and developments in the years after 1945.

Ideological differences and their effects

During the war, the Communist superpower, the USSR, had united with the capitalist superpower, the USA, to defeat fascism. However, Communism and capitalism were very different **ideologies** and economic systems, strongly opposed to one another. With Germany and Japan defeated, the reason for co-operation was gone. Differences of opinion began to emerge.

The USA

What were the main political and economic features of the USA?

- It had a democratic system of government. The President and **Congress** of the USA were chosen in free democratic elections.
- It had a capitalist economy. Business and property were privately owned. Individuals could make profits in business or move jobs if they wished. However, they might also go bankrupt or lose their jobs.
- The USA was the world's wealthiest country, but under capitalism there were always great contrasts – some people were very rich, others were very poor.
- Americans believed firmly in the freedom of the individual and in government by consent.

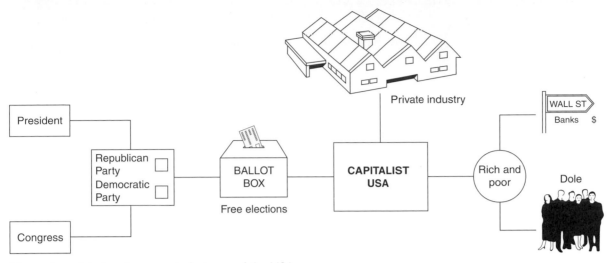

The main political and economic features of the USA.

In the 1920s and 1930s, the USA had followed a policy of **isolationism**. Now, faced by Communism extending into eastern Europe, the American Government was prepared to help and support people and countries that wanted democratic states with capitalist economies. This was seen as the defence of people's freedom against a system they did not want.

The USSR

The USSR was a Communist state.

- People could vote in elections for the **Supreme Soviet**, but they could only vote for members of the Communist Party and the Supreme Soviet had no real power. In the Communist system, people's lives were controlled closely.
- The rights of individuals were seen as less important than the good of society as a whole.
- The USSR had a planned economy. The Government owned all industry and planned what every factory should produce.
- Unlike the USA, the USSR had been attacked many times in the past. Germany had invaded Russia in 1914 and again in 1941, an attack which had been particularly vicious. Stalin was determined that this would never happen again. In his view, the USSR could only be safe if the countries on its borders were controlled by Communist governments. He believed that if he did not set up Communist governments, the USA would encourage hostile countries on the USSR's borders.

Key terms

Isolationism: withdrawing from international politics and policies.

Supreme Soviet: an elected body of representatives (the equivalent of the British Parliament), but which had no real power. It only met for two weeks a year. It was the Communist Party under Stalin that made the important decisions.

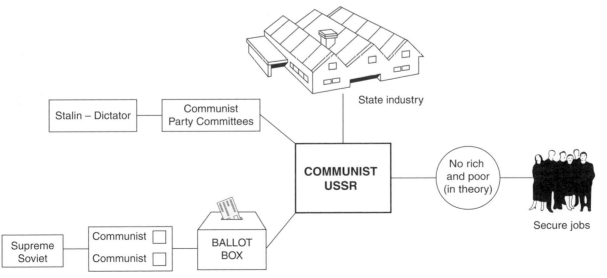

The main political and economic features of the USSR.

Revision tasks

1 Using the information on pages 36–37, choose six key words to summarise the USA's system of government. Then choose six key words to summarise the USSR's system of government.

2 Compare the two in a table with the following headings:

USA	USSR

Exam practice

1 Describe how ideological differences increased rivalry between the USA and the USSR in the years after 1945. *(4 marks)*

Exam tip Exam practice question 1 above is a Unit 1 question. Ensure you give a developed description using precise knowledge.

The Yalta and Potsdam Conferences

By early 1945, it was clear that Germany would be defeated. The minds of the Allied leaders turned to the problems that peace would bring. They held conferences at Yalta and Potsdam to discuss the challenges. These were:

- what to do with Germany and its leaders after surrender
- what was to happen to the occupied countries after they had been liberated, especially the countries of eastern Europe
- how to bring the war with Japan to a speedy end
- how to create and maintain a peace that would last.

The Yalta Conference, February 1945

At the Yalta Conference, the Allied leaders (Churchill, Roosevelt and Stalin) got on well together. The following points were agreed.

- Germany would be divided into four zones. These would be run by the USA, France, Britain and the USSR.
- Germany's capital city, Berlin (which was in the Soviet zone), would also be divided into four zones.
- The countries of eastern Europe would be allowed to hold free elections to decide how they would be governed.
- The USSR would join in the war against Japan in return for territory in Manchuria and Sakhalin Island.

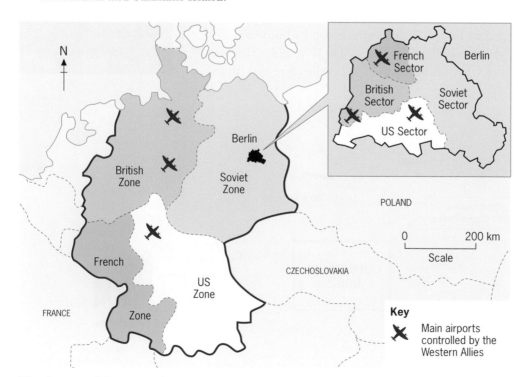

The division of Germany after the war.

The Potsdam Conference, July–August 1945

In April 1945, President Roosevelt died, so at the
Potsdam Conference, the USA was represented by a new
President, Harry Truman. During the conference,
Churchill was replaced by Clement Attlee as British Prime
Minister. The new leaders did not get on as well with
Stalin as Roosevelt and Churchill had done.

Attlee   Truman   Stalin

The discussions from the Yalta Conference were
continued at Potsdam. There was agreement on some points.

- The Nazi Party was to be banned and its leaders would be tried as war criminals.
- The Oder–Neisse (two rivers) line was to form part of the border between
  Poland and Germany.

However, there were disagreements on other issues. There were clear signs that
Stalin did not trust the USA and Britain and that they did not trust him.

1 Britain and the USA denied Stalin a naval base in the Mediterranean.
  - They saw no need for Stalin to have such a base.
  - Stalin saw this as evidence that his allies mistrusted him.

2 Stalin wanted more reparations from Germany than Britain and the USA did.
  - The USA and Britain did not wish to cripple Germany; they had seen the
    results of harsh reparations after the First World War.
  - Stalin was suspicious about why his allies seemed to want to protect
    Germany and even help it recover.

3 Stalin had set up a Communist government in Lublin, then the capital of
  Poland. Britain preferred the non-Communist Polish Government, which had
  lived in exile in Britain throughout the war. Truman and Attlee were very
  suspicious of Stalin's motives in setting up a Communist government.

> **Exam tip** Candidates
> often confuse the key
> features of these two
> conferences. Make sure you
> know who attended and
> what was agreed at each
> conference.

Revision tasks

1 Draw up a table on the Yalta and Potsdam Conferences like the one below. Add
  notes on what was agreed/where there was disagreement.

Conference	Points agreed	Areas of disagreement
Yalta		
Potsdam		

2 What important changes had occurred between the Yalta and the Potsdam
  Conferences?

The atom bomb and its effects

The Battle of Midway in May 1942 gave the USA control of the war in the Pacific.
However, although the Japanese were pushed back by US forces in 1943 and 1944
the American losses were huge due to the Japanese troops' refusal to surrender.
Consequently, the USA decided to use atom bombs to end the war against
Japan. On 6 August, the first bomb was used on Hiroshima and at least 75,000
people died instantly. Tens of thousands more died from radiation poisoning in
the following years. The second was dropped on Nagasaki three days later, with
60,000 casualties.

Stalin had been told about the atom bomb by Truman at the start of the
Potsdam Conference and was furious that it had been kept a secret. The use of the
atom bomb increased rivalry between the superpowers:

- Stalin was convinced that the USA used the bombs as a warning to the USSR.
- An arms race emerged with the USSR determined to develop its own atom bomb.

The 'Iron Curtain' and eastern Europe

In the years after 1945, Europe became divided into East and West. The countries of eastern Europe became Soviet **satellite states**.

Soviet expansion in the East

The Soviet Red Army advanced through large areas of eastern Europe whilst driving back the Germans. One year after the war, many Soviet troops were still stationed in much of eastern Europe.

Elections were held in each eastern European country, as promised at Yalta in 1945, but the evidence suggests they were rigged to allow the USSR-backed Communist parties to take control. In Bulgaria, Albania, Poland, Romania and Hungary, opponents of the Communists were beaten, murdered or frightened into submission. By 1948, all eastern European states had Communist governments.

Europe was now divided – East and West. In 1946, Churchill called this division the 'Iron Curtain'. Churchill said:

> *From Stettin on the Baltic to Trieste on the Adriatic, an iron curtain has descended across the continent. Behind that line lie all the capitals of central and eastern Europe ... and all are subject to a very high measure of control from Moscow.*

The spread of Communism, 1945–48.

Czechoslovakia, 1948

Czechoslovakia was not fully part of Stalin's 'Eastern Bloc' of countries – Communists were not fully in control. In the spring of 1948, elections were due and it seemed likely that the Communists would do badly, while the opposition would do well.

Communists organised marches and protests. Non-Communist ministers resigned and Foreign Minister Jan Masaryk was killed – probably murdered. In May 1948, elections took place but only Communists were allowed to stand. Czechoslovakia was now fully part of the Communist Eastern Bloc.

Key term

Satellite state: a country under the influence or control of another state.

Comment

Stalin was simply carrying out his policy of making sure he had friendly governments on his doorstep. However, to the British and Americans, he seemed to be trying to build up a Communist empire.

Revision tasks

1 What is meant by:
   ● the 'Iron Curtain
   ● satellite states?

2 Make a copy of the table below. In no more than one sentence, summarise the views of each side about Soviet expansion in eastern Europe.

	Soviet expansion in eastern Europe
Soviet view	
US view	

The Truman Doctrine, 1947

In 1947, the USA committed itself to a policy of containment of Communism in Europe.

Greece

You can see from the map on page 40 that Greece appeared to be next in line in the spread of Communism. Greek resistance against the Germans had been divided into two movements – the royalists (who wanted the return of the king) and the Communists. After the war, the royalists restored the king with the help of British troops. However, they came under attack from Communist forces and British troops withdrew. Greece asked the USA for help in early 1947.

Truman was already very worried about the spread of Communism. Under a foreign policy initiative that became known as the Truman Doctrine, the USA provided Greece with arms, supplies and money. The Communists were defeated in 1949 after a civil war.

Turkey

At the end of the Second World War, Stalin demanded partial control of the Dardanelles, a strategic passage between the Black Sea and the Mediterranean, which belonged to Turkey. As with Greece, British assistance to Turkey ended in 1947 and the USA dispatched military aid, including the aircraft carrier *Franklin D Roosevelt*, to ensure that Turkey would retain chief control of the passage.

The development of the Truman Doctrine

Events in Greece and Turkey convinced Truman that unless he acted, Communism would continue to spread. He therefore explained his policy to the world. This became known as the Truman Doctrine. Truman said:

> *I believe it must be the policy of the USA to support all free people who are resisting attempted subjugation by armed minorities or by outside pressure.*

- The USA would not return to isolationism – it would play a leading role in the world.
- The aim was to contain (stop the spread of) Communism but not to push it back. This became the policy of **containment**.

The Marshall Plan

The USA also became committed to the economic recovery of western Europe in order to prevent the spread of Communism.

Marshall Aid

Truman believed that poverty and hardship provided a breeding ground for Communism, so he wanted to make Europe prosperous again. It was also important for American businesses to have trading partners in the future, yet Europe's economies were still in ruins after the war.

The American Secretary of State, George Marshall, therefore visited Europe and came up with a European recovery programme – usually known as the Marshall Plan or Marshall Aid. This had two main aims:

- to stop the spread of Communism (although Truman did not admit this at the time)
- to help the economies of Europe to recover (this would eventually provide a market for American exports).

Key term

Containment: a foreign policy aimed at containing the political influence or military power of another country – for example, US policy to stop the spread of Communism during the Cold War.

Comment

Marshall Aid was a generous gesture by the USA but it was not entirely an act of kindness. Stalin saw it as an attempt by American business to dominate western Europe. If the USA was determined to 'buy' western Europe with its dollars, then he was determined to control eastern Europe with his Communist allies and the Red Army.

Effects of Marshall Aid

Between 12 and 13 billion dollars poured into Europe in the years 1947–51, providing vital help for Europe's economic recovery. However, Marshall Aid also caused tensions:

- Only 16 European countries accepted it – and these were all western European states.
- Stalin refused Marshall Aid for the USSR and banned eastern European countries from accepting it. Instead, he created his own organisations known as Cominform and Comecon.

Soviet response

Cominform, 1947

In 1947, Stalin set up Cominform – an alliance of Communist countries – probably as a response to the Marshall Plan. Its aim was to spread Communist ideas, but it also helped Stalin tighten his hold on his Communist allies because it restricted their contact with the West.

Only one Communist leader, Marshall Tito of Yugoslavia, was not prepared to accept Stalin's total leadership. He split with Moscow. However, Yugoslavia remained Communist.

Comecon, 1949

Set up by Stalin to co-ordinate the production and trade of the eastern European countries, it was like an early Communist version of the European Community. However, Comecon favoured the USSR more than any of its other members.

The Berlin Blockade and Airlift, 1948–49

This was the first major crisis of the Cold War.

Causes

At the end of the Second World War, the Allies divided Germany and Berlin into zones (see map on page 38). Germany's economy and government had been shattered by the war and the Allies were faced with a serious question: should they continue to occupy Germany or should they try to rebuild it?

- Britain and the USA wanted Germany to recover – they could not afford to keep feeding its people and they felt that punishing Germany would not help future peace.
- The French were unsure about whether to get Germany back on its feet or to 'ram home its defeat'.
- The USSR did not want to rebuild Germany and Stalin was suspicious about why the USA and Britain did.

In 1948, the French, American and British zones merged to become one zone, 'Trizonia' (in August 1949 this area became known as West Germany). With the help of Marshall Aid, West Germany began to recover and prosper. It was a very different story in East Germany. In this area, controlled by the USSR, there was poverty and hunger. Many East Germans were leaving because West Germany seemed a much more attractive place to live.

In Stalin's eyes, it seemed that the Allies were building up West Germany in order to attack him. When in 1948 they introduced a new West German currency (the Deutsche Mark), it was the last straw.

Exam tip Candidates often confuse the Truman Doctrine and the Marshall Plan. Ensure you have a thorough knowledge of both. Remember the Truman Doctrine is about political aid to western Europe to contain the spread of communism and the Marshall Plan is economic aid.

Exam tip Candidates often confuse this crisis with the crisis over the Berlin Wall in 1961. An easy way to remember the difference is 'B' for blockade comes before 'W' for wall.

Events

Stalin tried to blockade Berlin, the former capital of Germany, which was in East Germany (see map on page 38). In a month, he closed all road and rail connections from Berlin to West Germany, hoping he could force the western Allies out of the city. For many people at the time, it seemed there was a real risk of war. The USA and Britain faced a choice.

- They could withdraw from Berlin – but this would be humiliating and it might encourage Stalin to think he could invade West Germany.
- They could lift supplies into West Berlin by air – they had the planes but it would be risky as they might be shot down.

The Allies decided to airlift supplies. The airlift lasted until the following spring of 1949 and reached its peak on 16–17 April when 1,398 flights landed nearly 13,000 tonnes of supplies in 24 hours. During the airlift West Berliners were supplied with everything from food and clothing to oil and building supplies. It was a great success.

Results

By May 1949, the USSR lifted the blockade. It was a victory for the West, but relations with the USSR hit rock bottom. Co-operation in Germany in the future was very unlikely and the country would remain divided. The zones controlled by the USA, Britain and France became the Federal Republic of Germany (West Germany) in August 1949. In October 1949, the Soviet zone became the German Democratic Republic (East Germany).

Revision tasks

1 The Truman Doctrine and Marshall Plan were described as being two sides of the same coin.

Make your own copy of both sides of this imaginary coin. On one side, give a brief definition of the Truman Doctrine. On the other side, write a brief definition of the Marshall Plan.

2 Draw a flow chart to show the causes, events and results of the Berlin crisis of 1948–49.

3 How far do you feel each side was to blame for the tension after the Second World War? Decide where you would put the USA and the USSR on the scale below:

Mostly to blame  Not to blame

4 Draw up a table like the one below. Use the information in this chapter to complete it.

Organisation	Members	Purpose	Effects on East–West relations
Marshall Plan			
Comecon			
Cominform			

Exam practice

1 Which was the more important reason for the development of the Cold War in the years 1945–49?
- Soviet expansion in eastern Europe
- The Truman Doctrine

You must refer to **both** reasons in your answer.
(10 marks)

2 **Source 1** suggests possible reasons for the Cold War. Do you agree that these were the main reasons?
(6 marks)

SOURCE 1

A US cartoon of 1946 showing the USSR as a bear taking over eastern Europe.

Exam tip Exam practice question 1 above is a Unit 1 question. Make sure you refer to both reasons in your answer and come to a judgement. You could decide that both reasons were of equal importance.

Exam tip: q2 Explain your answer by referring to:
- the purpose of the source – what is it trying to make you believe?
- its content – what is it suggesting about the reasons for the Cold War?
- your own contextual knowledge – in other words, what do you know about the beginning of the Cold War?

4.2 How did the Cold War develop in the years 1949–60?

The Cold War intensified in the years after 1949 with the formation of rival alliance systems and the outbreak of the Korean War.

NATO (The North Atlantic Treaty Organisation), 1949

This military alliance contained most of the states in western Europe as well as the USA and Canada. Its main purpose was to defend each of its members. If one member was attacked, all the others would help to defend it. When the USSR developed its own atomic bomb in 1949, NATO seemed even more important to the defence of western Europe, since at the time no western European country had atomic weapons.

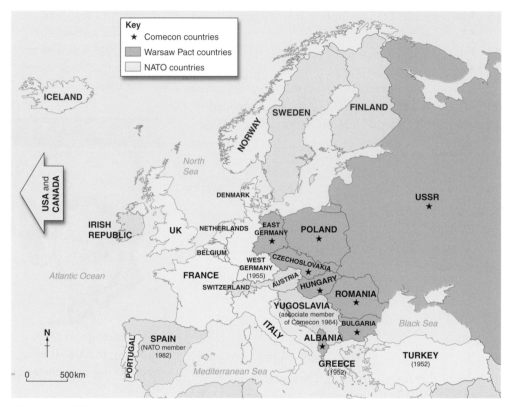

Alliances, 1949–55.

The importance of NATO

- The USA was now formally committed to the defence of western Europe.
- Stalin did not see it as a defensive alliance but as a direct threat to the USSR.
- The USA was able to build air bases in western Europe where planes armed with nuclear weapons could be stationed ready for use against the USSR.

> **Exam tip** Questions on NATO are often not well answered as candidates fail to revise its features and importance. Ensure you revise these thoroughly.

The nuclear arms race

- During 1945–49, the USA was the only country to possess atomic weapons.
- In 1949, the USSR successfully tested an atomic bomb.
- In 1952, the USA detonated its first hydrogen bomb.
- In 1953, the USSR tested its own hydrogen bomb.

By 1953, the USSR appeared to be catching up with the USA in the developing arms race. The balance tilted even more in the direction of the USSR when China became communist in October 1949. In 1950, Stalin and the new Chinese Communist leader, Mao Zedong, signed a 30-year treaty of friendship.

The Korean War

The outbreak of the Korean War meant that the Cold War had spread to Asia.

Reasons for US and UN involvement

Europe was not the only part of the world where the USSR came into conflict with the USA. Stalin was supporting Communists in Asia – the new Communist Government in China as well as communist groups in other Asian countries. The Americans thought that they were seeing the eastern European story being repeated in Asia and were determined to prevent the further spread of Communism in the region.

The crisis came in Korea. At the end of the Second World War, the USSR had taken control of North Korea and set up a Communist state. In the south, the Americans set up a government that was supposed to be a democracy, although it relied heavily on military backing. The South Korean president (Syngman Rhee) and the North Korean president (Kim Il Sung) each claimed to be President of all Korea. Relations were tense. In June 1950, North Korea invaded South Korea.

Events

- The North Korean forces pushed back the South Korean forces into a small area of south-east Korea around Pusan (see Map 1 below). President Truman asked the **United Nations** to help and the Security Council's permanent members agreed to do so. (Normally, the USSR would have exercised its veto, but it was boycotting UN meetings in protest at the refusal to admit Communist China into the UN.)
- UN forces from many countries (but mainly America) drove the Communists back almost as far as the Yalu River on the border with China (see Map 2).
- This worried China who did not want a non-Communist neighbour supported by US troops. China joined the war.
- The UN forces were driven back (see Map 3) and the UN commander, General MacArthur, called for the use of the atomic bomb. President Truman sacked MacArthur.
- Once again, UN troops began to push back the Communists. By June 1951, the fighting seemed to be settling roughly around the **38th parallel** (see Map 4).
- In 1953, a truce was agreed at Panmunjom (on the 38th parallel).

> ### Key terms
> **United Nations (UN):** an international peace-keeping force set up after the Second World War.
> **The 38th parallel:** the border between North and South Korea from 1945 to June 1950.

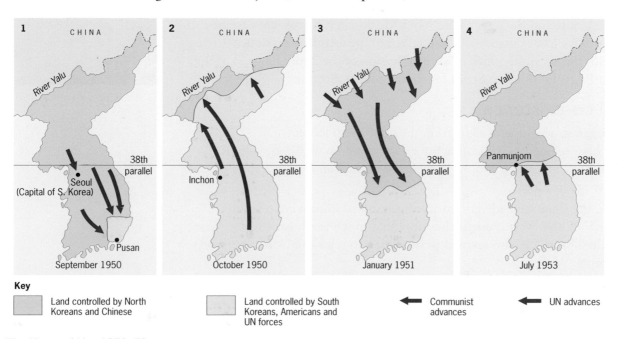

Key

| | Land controlled by North Koreans and Chinese | | Land controlled by South Koreans, Americans and UN forces | ← Communist advances | ← UN advances |

The Korean War, 1950–53.

Consequences

When China became a Communist country in 1949, the USA was extremely worried. Chinese–American relations were strained for many years. President Truman worried that the **domino effect** would work in Asia as it had in Europe.

So the USA was pleased with the result in Korea. The Americans saw the Korean War as an example of successful containment. However, it had been achieved at a price. There was massive damage to Korea itself. In addition, many observers thought that the USA had used the UN for its own purposes. To this day, there are two states in Korea and relations are very strained.

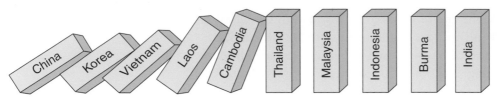

The domino effect.

'The Thaw'

In the mid-1950s, there was some improvement in relations between the USA and the USSR.

Khrushchev

Stalin died in 1953. There was a subsequent power struggle to succeed him as leader of the USSR and the victor was Nikita Khrushchev. Khrushchev seemed to be a less aggressive leader than Stalin and talked of '**peaceful co-existence**' (living in peace) with the West. In 1956, in a closed session of the 20th Congress of the Communist Party, he attacked Stalin for having been a dictator.

Peaceful co-existence

The West began to see hopeful signs from the new Soviet leader.
- Khrushchev seemed to be encouraging greater freedom within the USSR.
- On a visit to Warsaw in 1956, he indicated that the Polish people should be allowed more freedom.

Up to 1956, the signs seemed very positive in terms of improving relations between the East and West. Khrushchev appeared much less hostile to the West than Stalin had been. He also seemed to be willing to relax the USSR's grip on eastern Europe.

Austria

In 1955, the Soviets agreed to sign the Austrian State Treaty, ending the occupation of Austria that had continued since 1945. Austria had been divided into four zones at the end of the Second World War and the Soviets had taken many food supplies in reparations from their zone. This now came to an end: Austria became independent and her 1937 frontiers were restored.

The Warsaw Pact

Although Khrushchev believed in peaceful co-existence, he was determined to strengthen eastern Europe in the face of NATO. He was especially annoyed by the decision to integrate the Federal Republic of Germany (West Germany) into NATO in 1955.

After West Germany joined NATO, the Soviet response was to set up the Warsaw Pact – a Communist version of NATO. The Soviets had not forgotten the damage that Germany had inflicted on the USSR in the Second World War.

Hungary, 1956

Peaceful co-existence did not put an end to Soviet repression in eastern Europe, which was shown by the Soviet reaction to events in Hungary in 1956. An attempted uprising was brutally crushed by the USSR.

Causes of the uprising

Hungary had been treated as a defeated country by the Soviets after the Second World War. With the support of the USSR, a Communist government had been established under Rákosi, who closely followed Stalin's rules. The Hungarians hated Rákosi and his secret police (the AVH) because of the brutality they had shown, executing or imprisoning thousands of opponents. There were protests against the falling standard of living and increased poverty, which Hungarians blamed on Soviet policies.

Events

The protests got worse and Stalin's statue was pulled down and dragged through the streets of Budapest. Rákosi was forced to resign and Soviet tanks moved in. Nagy became Prime Minister and Soviet troops withdrew. Nagy was determined on reform. He wanted free elections, the end of the secret police, and the removal of the Soviet army of occupation.

However, Khrushchev became alarmed when Nagy demanded the right for Hungary to withdraw from the Warsaw Pact and follow a neutral role in the Cold War. This was too much for the USSR. Free elections could mean the end of Communism in Hungary. If Hungary withdrew from the Warsaw Pact, there would be a gap in the Iron Curtain; the Soviet buffer zone with the West would be broken.

Soviet troops and 1,000 tanks moved into Hungary to crush the uprising. Nagy appealed to the West for help but none came. Two weeks of street fighting followed but the Hungarians were no match for the Soviet forces. Nagy was captured and later shot.

Comment

All of the alliances demonstrated the fear and mistrust that brought about the Cold War. The western democracies and the USSR both feared the rise of another state like Nazi Germany. However, each side saw the other as this potential threat, certainly not itself. The creation of alliances for self-defence could very easily look like an alliance preparing to attack.

Results

- Between 2,500 and 30,000 Hungarians, mostly civilians, were killed along with 700 Soviet troops. Over 200,000 refugees fled Hungary and settled in the West.
- The uprising highlighted the limitations of Khrushchev's policy of peaceful co-existence.
- There was no active support for the rising in the West. This was because Britain, France and the USA were preoccupied with the Suez crisis.
- A new pro-Soviet Government was set up under János Kádár. Kádár re-established Communist control of Hungary and negotiated the withdrawal of Soviet troops once the crisis was over.
- Other satellite states in eastern Europe did not dare to challenge Soviet authority after the events in Hungary.

Revision task

Make a copy of the table below and summarise the part played in the Hungarian uprising by each person.

	Part played in Hungarian uprising
Nagy	
Khrushchev	
Kádár	
Rákosi	

The space and arms races

The late 1950s and early 1960s saw increasing competition between the superpowers in space exploration and the development of nuclear weapons.

The space race

The two superpowers used the space race to try to demonstrate the superiority of either capitalism or Communism. At first, the USSR took the lead. In the later 1950s, it launched the first satellite, known as Sputnik I, and put the first man in space, Yuri Gagarin. This alarmed the USA, who seemed to be lagging behind in space technology. Subsequently, however, it was the USA who took the lead in the space race with the Apollo missions that eventually landed the first man on the moon, Neil Armstrong, in 1969.

The arms race

The space race, in turn, intensified the arms race. The launch of Sputnik I in 1957 showed that the Soviets had developed rockets that could carry nuclear warheads capable of reaching the USA. In retaliation, the USA developed its own Inter-Continental Ballistic Missiles (ICBMs) in 1957 and, by 1959, these could be stored underground and be ready for use in 30 seconds. Moreover, the firing of a Polaris missile from a nuclear submarine by the USA in 1960 demonstrated that a missile could be fired from the sea close to the USSR and therefore would be more accurate.

Comment

The Suez crisis was a war fought by Britain, France and Israel against Egypt in October 1956. It followed the decision by the President of Egypt, Nasser, to nationalise the Suez Canal. Both the USA and the USSR objected to the attack on Egypt and forced Britain, France and Israel to withdraw.

Exam practice

1 Describe how the USSR dealt with the Hungarian uprising.
(4 marks)

Exam tip Exam practice question 1 above is a Unit 1 question. Ensure you give a developed description that uses precise knowledge.

Exam tip You will need to know some details of the space and arms races, particularly how each increased rivalry between the USA and the USSR.

Comment

The Polaris missile was a Submarine-Launched Ballistic Missile (SLBM) carrying a nuclear warhead developed during the Cold War for the US Navy. It was gradually replaced by the Poseidon missile from 1972 onwards.

Key content

You need to have a good working knowledge of the following areas.
Tick off each item once you are confident in your knowledge.

- ❑ The ideological differences between the USA and the USSR
- ❑ The key features of the Yalta and Potsdam Conferences
- ❑ The dropping of the atom bomb and its effects
- ❑ The Iron Curtain and Soviet expansion in eastern Europe
- ❑ The Truman Doctrine and the Marshall Plan
- ❑ The Berlin Blockade and Airlift
- ❑ The formation of NATO, its membership and purpose
- ❑ The nuclear arms race
- ❑ The causes, events and results of the Korean War
- ❑ 'The Thaw' and peaceful co-existence
- ❑ The Warsaw Pact
- ❑ The causes, events and results of the Hungarian uprising of 1956
- ❑ The continuation of the space and arms races of the 1950s.

Check your knowledge online with our Quick quizzes at www.hodderplus.co.uk/modernworldhistory.

Chapter 5: Crises of the Cold War and Détente, 1960–1980

In the years 1960–70, there were a number of crises involving the USA and the USSR, each of which intensified Cold War rivalry. The most serious were the U-2 crisis of 1960, the Cuban missile crisis of 1962 and the Soviet invasion of Czechoslovakia in 1968. In the 1970s, there were real attempts to improve relations with a policy of Détente, but these were ultimately unsuccessful due to the Soviet invasion of Afghanistan in 1979.

Key issues

As with all examination topics, you will be expected to do more than simply learn the content and write it out again. You will need to show understanding of key issues from the period. These are:

- How close to war was the world in the 1960s?
- Why did Détente develop and collapse in the 1970s?

5.1 How close to war was the world in the 1960s?

In the 1960s there were a number of crises involving the USA and the USSR, each of which intensified the Cold War rivalry, with the most serious of these being the Cuban missile crisis of 1962.

The U-2 crisis, 1960

On 1 May 1960, another incident occurred that developed into a crisis. The Soviets shot down an American U-2 spy plane over the USSR and captured the pilot, Gary Powers. According to the Soviets, he admitted he was on a spying mission.

The U-2 had been developed by the US Central Intelligence Agency (CIA). It was able to fly at high altitudes and was equipped with powerful cameras and radio receivers enabling it to detect Soviet long-range bomber bases and missile sites.

The American Government denied that spying flights took place over Soviet territory and claimed that Gary Powers had accidentally strayed into Soviet airspace whilst on a flight to study weather conditions. The Soviets were keen to show the world that the American Government was lying so they developed the film taken by Powers on his mission, which showed he had clearly been spying. This severely embarrassed the American Government.

Khrushchev demanded that the Americans:

- apologise for the U-2 affair
- stop future spying flights
- punish those responsible.

President Eisenhower agreed to stop spying flights but refused to apologise. Khrushchev then walked out of the Paris Summit Conference that took place in May 1960 between the leaders of the USA, the USSR, France and Britain. This conference was supposed to achieve improved relations between East and West by discussing arms limitation and the possible reunification of Germany.

Gary Powers was sentenced to ten years in prison in the USSR, but was exchanged in 1962 for a Soviet agent.

The incident was especially damaging for President Eisenhower.

- Not only had an American plane been shot down spying over Soviet territory but the Americans had lied about it for all the world to see.
- The Soviets had scored a propaganda victory.

The U-2 affair showed how quickly conflict between the superpowers could develop from a single incident. The results in terms of Cold War relations were extremely serious.

The situation in Berlin

In 1961, the Cold War reached another turning point with the construction of the Berlin Wall.

Contrasts in Berlin

Berlin had always been a source of conflict between the Soviets and western Allies. Capitalist West Berlin, surrounded by the Communist state of East Germany, continued to be a problem for East Germany and the USSR.

- The high standard of living enjoyed by the people of West Berlin contrasted sharply with that of the Communist half of the city – East Berlin. It was a continual reminder to the people in East Germany of their poor living conditions.
- It was estimated that 3 million people had crossed from East to West Berlin between 1946 and 1960. Many of these people were skilled workers and it seemed that the economic survival of East Germany was in doubt if this escape route remained open.

The building of the Wall

In 1961, Khrushchev and the East German leadership decided to act. Without warning, on 13 August 1961, the East Germans began to build a wall surrounding West Berlin.

- At first, the structure was little more than a barbed wire fence, but by 17 August it was replaced with a stone wall.
- All movement between East and West was stopped.
- For several days, Soviet and American tanks faced each other across divided Berlin streets.

The building of the Berlin Wall had some immediate effects.

- The flow of refugees was reduced to a trickle.
- Western nations won a propaganda victory since it appeared that Communist states needed to build walls to prevent their citizens from leaving.

However, the western nations had to be satisfied with a propaganda victory only. It was clear that the USA and NATO were not going to try to stop the building of the wall. In reality, there was little the western powers could do to stop it.

A section of the Berlin Wall near the Brandenburg Gate, c. 1965.

Kennedy's response

From the 1960s until the 1980s, the Berlin Wall became a symbol of the division between the capitalist West and the Communist East. American President John F. Kennedy made a historic visit to West Berlin and declared that the city was a symbol of the struggle between the forces of freedom and the Communist world. For the USSR and East Germany, however, the wall was simply an economic and political necessity. The loss of so many refugees from East Germany had been threatening the very existence of the state.

> ## Revision task
>
> What part did the following play in the space and arms races?
> **a)** Sputnik
> **b)** Polaris
> **c)** ICBMs

Exam practice

1 Which reason was more important for worsening relations between the USA and the USSR in the early 1960s?
- the U-2 crisis
- the building of the Berlin Wall

You must refer to **both** reasons in your answer. *(10 marks)*

Exam tip Exam practice question 1 above is a Unit 1 question. Make sure you refer to both reasons in your answer and come to a judgement. You could decide that both reasons were of equal importance.

The nuclear deterrent

There were further Cold War crises in the 1960s, including the Cuban missile crisis and the Soviet invasion of Czechoslovakia.

The Cuban missile crisis highlighted the possibility of nuclear conflict. By the end of the 1960s, the superpowers had enough nuclear weapons to destroy the world. However this, in itself, acted as a nuclear deterrent and became known as Mutually Assured Destruction (MAD). No side would dare strike first when it knew the attack would inevitably lead to its own destruction.

The Cuban missile crisis, 1962

The Cuban missile crisis was the most serious conflict between the USSR and the USA in the history of the Cold War. Cuba was a Communist country just 144 kilometres off the coast of the USA. In October 1962, American spy planes identified nuclear missile sites being built on Cuba.

Castro and Cuba

Cuba had become Communist after a takeover by Fidel Castro in 1958. He was popular in Cuba, in part because he gave land seized from wealthy Americans to the Cuban people.

The USA had retaliated by cutting off aid to Cuba, and refused to buy Castro's cotton and tobacco. In return, Castro secured help from the USSR. Khrushchev was keen to gain influence in Cuba, close to the USA's south-eastern coastline.

In spring 1961, the USA had a new President, John F. Kennedy. He was alarmed at what he saw as a Communist threat on the USA's doorstep. He gave American support to an invasion of Cuba by rebels opposed to Castro's Government. The landing took place at the Bay of Pigs, and was a disaster. There was no popular support for it in Cuba.

Events of the crisis

The crisis lasted for thirteen days.

16 October	*Kennedy was told that Khrushchev intended to build missile sites on Cuba.*
18–19 October	*Kennedy held talks with his closest advisers. The 'Hawks' wanted an aggressive policy whilst the 'Doves' favoured a peaceful solution.*
20 October	*Kennedy decided to impose a naval **blockade** around Cuba to prevent Soviet missiles reaching Cuba. The Americans searched any ship suspected of carrying arms or missiles.*
21 October	*Kennedy made a broadcast to the American people, informing them of the potential threat and what he intended to do.*
23 October	*Khrushchev sent a letter to Kennedy insisting that Soviet ships would force their way through the blockade.*

Key term

Blockade: cutting off a place by surrounding it with troops or ships.

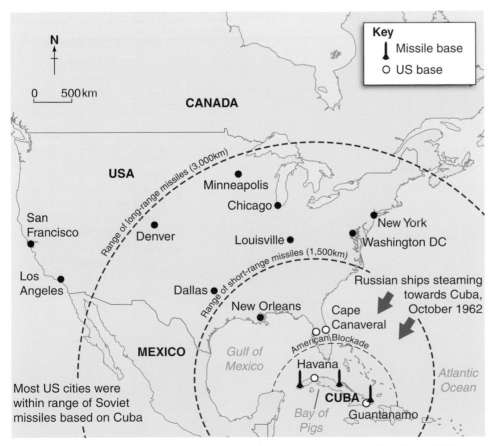

The position and threat of Cuban missiles, and the crisis at its peak, October 1962.

24 October	*Khrushchev issued a statement insisting that the USSR would use nuclear weapons in the event of a war.*
25 October	*Kennedy wrote to Khrushchev asking him to withdraw missiles from Cuba.*
26 October	*Khrushchev replied to Kennedy's letter. He said he would withdraw the missiles if the USA promised not to invade Cuba and withdrew its missiles from Turkey.*
27 October	*A US spy plane was shot down over Cuba. Attorney General Robert Kennedy (brother of the President) agreed a deal with the USSR. The USA would withdraw missiles from Turkey as long as it was kept secret.*
28 October	*Khrushchev accepted the deal.*

Results of the crisis

The Cuban crisis had a major effect on East–West relations.

- Leaders of both the USSR and the USA realised that nuclear war had been a real possibility and it was vital that a similar crisis should not happen again.
- The Americans and Soviets decided to set up a telephone link (or 'hot line') so that direct communication could take place in future between Washington and Moscow. Nuclear arms talks also began and, in 1963, a Test Ban Treaty was signed between the USA, the USSR and Britain.

President Kennedy became an instant hero in the West for his apparent tough handling of the Soviets.

Exam tip The Cuban missile crisis is a popular exam topic. Ensure you thoroughly revise the causes, events and results.

Comment

In some ways, the Cuban missile crisis was the height of Cold War tension. Never before had the world been so close to nuclear conflict as it was in October 1962. However, the crisis resulted in arms reductions and improved communications (if not better relations) between the USA and the USSR.

Revision tasks

1 Make a copy of the table below. Summarise the part played by the following people in the Cuban missile crisis.

Fidel Castro	
John Kennedy	
Robert Kennedy	
Nikita Khrushchev	

2 Place the following events of the crisis in the correct chronological order:
   - American spy plane shot down over Cuba
   - the USA blockades Cuba
   - Khrushchev accepts the deal
   - the US discovers Soviet missile sites on Cuba
   - Robert Kennedy agrees a deal.

3 Which country do you think gained the most from the crisis: the USA, the USSR or Cuba? Explain your answer.

Exam practice

1 Describe how the USA and the USSR reached a solution over the Cuban missile crisis.

(4 marks)

Exam tip Exam practice question 1 above is a Unit 1 question. Ensure you give a developed description with precise knowledge. You will need to describe two key features. Remember key features can include causes, events or results.

Czechoslovakia, 1968

In 1968, the USSR once again showed its unwillingness to allow greater freedom in the Eastern Bloc.

The Prague Spring

In 1967, Alexander Dubček became Communist Party Secretary in Czechoslovakia. In the spring of 1968 (the 'Prague Spring'), Dubček began to reform the Communist system.

- Censorship of the press was ended.
- Other political parties apart from the Communist Party were allowed.
- Some political prisoners were released and Czech citizens were given greater freedom to travel abroad.

The reforms in Czechoslovakia became known as 'socialism with a human face'. They seemed to represent the general easing of tension between East and West that had taken place after the Cuban crisis.

The reaction of the USSR

However, Dubček's reforms were seen as a major threat by the new leader of the USSR, Brezhnev. As in Hungary twelve years earlier, action was taken to prevent the reforms from sweeping the Communists out of power in Czechoslovakia and spreading to the rest of eastern Europe.

- In August 1968, 400,000 Warsaw Pact troops entered Czechoslovakia, arrested leading reformers and seized key towns and cities.
- Dubček and the Czech President Svovoda were flown to Moscow where they talked with Brezhnev for four days.
- On 27 August, the Czech leaders returned and announced that many of their reforms were to be stopped and censorship re-introduced. In 1969, Dubček resigned and was replaced by a loyal Communist, Husak.

As with Hungary in 1956, the western powers did little to assist those in conflict with the Soviet leadership. Both China and the West condemned Soviet action in Czechoslovakia, but did nothing to support Dubček and his Government.

The Brezhnev Doctrine

After the failure of the Czechs to gain more freedom from Soviet control, the new Czech leader, Husak, set about returning to the old ways. The reforms of the Prague Spring were reversed, and the USSR was once more firmly in control of Czech policy.

Brezhnev then set out what became known as the Brezhnev Doctrine. He argued that a threat to one socialist (that is, Communist) country was a threat to them all. (This doctrine clearly echoed the Truman Doctrine of 1947 and the American fear of the domino effect, see pages 41 and 46.) However, he went on to say that force would be used whenever necessary to keep the Soviet satellites firmly under Soviet influence.

This doctrine and the Soviet actions in Czechoslovakia in 1968 did nothing to improve relations between the USSR and the USA. Yet, in spite of it, there was a thaw in relations very quickly in what has become known as the process of **Détente**.

> ## Comment
>
> *The end of the Prague Spring showed once again that the Soviet leadership would not tolerate reform in its satellite states and that the West was unwilling to risk nuclear war over eastern European countries.*

> ## Key term
>
> **Détente:** the relaxing of tension or hostility between nations – for example, the improvement of relations between the USA and the USSR at the end of the 1960s.

Revision task

Make a copy of the table below. Complete each section in note form. In the last column, make a judgement about how serious each crisis was on a scale of 1–5, with 5 being the most serious. Give a brief explanation for each decision.

Crisis	Causes	Events	Results	How serious (1–5)
The U-2 crisis				
The Berlin Wall				
The Cuban missile crisis				
The Prague Spring				

Exam practice

1 **Source 1** suggests possible consequences of the Cuban missile crisis. Do you agree that these were the main consequences? Explain your answer by referring to:
   - the purpose of the source – what is it trying to make you believe?
   - its content – what is it suggesting about the consequences of the Cuban missile crisis?
   - your own contextual knowledge – in other words, what do you know about the consequences of the Cuban missile crisis?
   (6 marks)

SOURCE 1
Extract from the memoirs of Khrushchev, published in 1971.
The Cuban missile crisis was a triumph for Soviet foreign policy and a personal triumph in my career. Today Cuba exists as an independent socialist country right in front of America. Cuba's existence is good propaganda. We behaved with dignity and forced the United States to demobilise and to recognise Cuba.

5.2 Why did Détente develop and collapse in the 1970s?

From the end of the 1960s and through much of the 1970s, there was a general easing of tension between the USA and the USSR as both sides realised the dangers of nuclear war and sought to reduce defence spending. This process became known as Détente and led to a series of agreements including **SALT** I in 1972, the Helsinki Agreement of 1975, and SALT II in 1979. Détente finally ended with the Soviet invasion of Afghanistan.

Key term

SALT: Strategic Arms Limitation Talks, which limited the number of nuclear weapons and warheads held by each side.

Reasons for Détente

This relaxation in relations was due to several reasons:
- The USA was keen on reducing its spending on arms. In addition, involvement in Vietnam had not gone well and, by 1968, the USA was seeking to end the war. Nixon had developed a policy called 'linkage' – the idea of offering concessions to the USSR such as arms reduction in exchange for Brezhnev persuading his North Vietnamese ally to negotiate an end to the war.
- The Soviet leader was keen to gain access to US technology and further grain sales. He also hoped to reach an agreement on arms limitations which would reduce spending on the arms race.
- China also influenced Détente. Nixon had visited China three months earlier. He hoped that closer relations with China might help to end the war in Vietnam, as the Chinese were close allies of the North Vietnamese. Brezhnev did not want to see a Chinese-US alliance develop, especially as relations between the USSR and China were strained. There seemed the possibility of a full-scale war between the two Communist states. In view of this, Brezhnev urgently needed to ease relations with the USA.
- There had been a small-scale Détente between East and West Germany. West Germany agreed in 1969 not to seek nuclear weapons. This laid to rest one of the greatest Soviet fears – a nuclear-armed West Germany.

The progress of Détente

There were several developments in Détente in the 1970s. The first Strategic Arms Limitation Treaty (SALT 1) was signed in 1972. The two superpowers agreed that there would be no further production of strategic ballistic missiles (short-range, lightweight missiles). They also agreed that submarines carrying nuclear weapons would only be introduced when existing stocks of Intercontinental Ballistic Missiles became obsolete. SALT I was significant because it was the first agreement between the superpowers that successfully limited the number of nuclear weapons they held.

There were also summit meetings between Brezhnev and Nixon. Nixon visited Moscow in 1972 where he made it clear that he did not see Vietnam as an obstacle to the process of Détente. Two years later Nixon again visited Moscow where the two leaders agreed they would continue to remove the danger of nuclear war, and limit and eventually end the arms race.

Nixon's visit to Moscow was followed by the Helsinki Agreements of 1975. The USA and the USSR, along with 33 other nations, made declarations about three distinct international issues:

- **Security.** The recognition of Europe's frontiers. The USSR accepted the existence of West Germany.
- **Co-operation.** There were calls for closer economic, scientific and cultural links.
- **Human rights.** They agreed to respect human rights and basic freedoms such as thought and speech.

Soviet involvement in Afghanistan

In December 1979, the USSR invaded Afghanistan. The Soviets insisted that they had been invited into Afghanistan to restore order, but western nations protested that it was a straightforward invasion that could not be justified. Despite worldwide protest, the invasion and occupation of Afghanistan continued.

Reasons for the invasion

The Soviets invaded Afghanistan for several reasons.

- They were concerned about the Muslim revolution in neighbouring Iran, which could have spread to Afghanistan and Muslim areas inside the USSR.
- The political situation in Afghanistan was very unstable at the end of the 1970s and the Soviets wanted to maintain their influence in the area.
- Afghanistan was close to the Middle East oil reserves of the western powers and the ports of the Indian Ocean. The Soviets wanted to develop their interests in this area.

Consequences

Within weeks of the invasion, Soviet troops were being killed by **Mujahadin** rebels, who used very effective guerrilla tactics. The USA secretly began to send very large shipments of money, arms and equipment to Pakistan and from there to the Mujahadin. The campaign became a nightmare for the USSR; unwinnable and a severe drain on their finances. The Soviet leader, Gorbachev, eventually withdrew troops in 1988 due to the excessive cost of the conflict.

President Carter was furious with the Soviet invasion and took action. He pulled the USA out

> **Exam tip** Candidates often lack precise knowledge of the key features of Détente in the 1970s. Ensure you revise this section thoroughly.

> **Key term**
>
> **Mujahadin:** Afghan tribesmen who fought against the Soviet invasion.

The importance of Afghanistan to the Soviets.

of the 1980 Moscow Olympic Games. (The USSR retaliated in 1984 by pulling out of the Los Angeles Games.) Carter told the Senate not to ratify (agree to) the SALT II treaty that was ready to sign and would have further limited the number of nuclear weapons. He also cut trade between the USA and the USSR – for example, he prevented food and technological goods, such as computers, being sold to the USSR.

Revision tasks

Using the information from pages 56–58 above, answer the following questions.

1 Using a mind map, summarise the reasons for Détente.

2 Make a copy of the table below. Complete each section in note form.

Key features of Détente	Describe this feature and how it helped improve relations
SALT 1	
Nixon–Brezhnev meetings	
Helsinki	

3 Give two reasons for the Soviet invasion of Afghanistan.

Exam practice

1 Describe how the Soviet invasion of Afghanistan ended the policy of Détente.

(4 marks)

Exam tip Exam practice question 1 above is a Unit 1 question. Ensure you give a developed description that uses precise knowledge. You will need to describe two key features. Remember key features can include causes, events or results.

Key content

You need to have a good working knowledge of the following areas. **Tick off each item** once you are confident in your knowledge.

❏ The U-2 crisis of 1960
❏ The reasons for and effects of the building of the Berlin Wall in 1961
❏ The nuclear deterrent and the space race of the 1960s
❏ The causes, events and results of the Cuban missile crisis
❏ The Prague Spring of 1968, the reactions of the USSR and the Brezhnev Doctrine
❏ Reasons for successes of Détente in the 1970s
❏ Reasons for and the effects of the Soviet invasion of Afghanistan

Check your knowledge online with our Quick quizzes at www.hodderplus.co.uk/modernworldhistory.

The Cold War resumed in the early 1980s under Reagan but came to an end in the late 1980s as Communism collapsed. However, in the 1990s the USA took on a new role and the UN faced a series of problems.

Key issues

As with all examination topics, you will be expected to do more than simply learn the content and write it out again. You will need to show understanding of key issues from the period. These are:

- Why did Communism collapse in central and eastern Europe?
- What problems faced the USA and the UN following the end of the Cold War?

6.1 Why did Communism collapse in central and eastern Europe?

The newly elected US president, Ronald Reagan, was keen to challenge the USSR and re-establish the USA as the leading superpower. This led to increased rivalry between the two superpowers.

Reagan and the renewal of the Cold War

The period following the Soviet invasion of Afghanistan is often described as the Second Cold War.

The 'evil empire'

Ronald Reagan succeeded Carter as President of the USA. He believed that Détente had been a disaster and rejected the idea of **peaceful co-existence** with the USSR. Instead he was determined to get tough and, in a speech in 1983, referred to the USSR as 'that evil empire'.

'Star Wars'

Reagan was convinced that the USA could win the Cold War. He believed that the USSR should be forced to disarm by his new initiative – SDI or the Strategic Defence Initiative, which was nicknamed 'Star Wars'. It was intended to be a satellite anti-missile system that would orbit the Earth to protect the USA from any Soviet missiles. Satellites equipped with powerful lasers would act as a 'nuclear umbrella' against Soviet nuclear weapons.

This was a turning point in the arms race. During Détente the two superpowers had been evenly matched. Now the balance was very much in favour of the USA. The USSR could not compete with SDI.

- The Soviet economy could not produce enough wealth to finance the development of new space-based weapons.
- The USSR was well behind the USA in the development of computers, essential for the 'Star Wars' programme.

> ### Key term
>
> **Peaceful co-existence:** the policy of co-operation rather than rivalry with the West.

Solidarity in Poland

In the early 1980s, the USSR had problems of its own in eastern Europe. In 1980, protest movements in Poland highlighted the high prices and the fuel and food shortages that the Polish people faced. Shipyard workers at Gdansk went on strike, led by Lech Walesa, an electrician, who founded Solidarity, the first free trade union within Communist eastern Europe. Pope John Paul II (himself a Pole) lent his support to the movement.

Nationwide strikes threatened to bring the country to a halt, and many Poles feared a Soviet invasion (as in Hungary in 1956 and Czechoslovakia in 1968). Ominously, the Soviet army began carrying out 'training manoeuvres' near the Polish border. Meanwhile, the Polish Communist leader, General Jaruzelski, decided to impose rule by the army. Political opponents were arrested, including Walesa, and Solidarity was declared to be illegal. The situation in Poland was still tense when Brezhnev died in 1982.

The situation in the USSR drifted. Brezhnev was followed by Yuri Andropov and then Constantin Chernenko. Both men suffered ill-health and died without achieving much.

The next President of the USSR, Mikhail Gorbachev, had a huge impact on the USSR, eastern Europe and the world. In Poland, Solidarity re-emerged, and by the late 1980s the Communist Government commanded little respect. Gorbachev was encouraging greater freedoms, both in the USSR and in the **satellite states**.

> ## Revision task
> Draw a mind map to summarise the key features of the Solidarity movement in Poland. Include reasons for the movement, the role of Lech Walesa, and the reactions of the Soviet and Polish Governments.

The effects of the Afghan war

The Soviet involvement in Afghanistan had worsened the economic and political problems of the USSR:

- The USSR was locked in a costly and unwinnable war.
- The economy was weak with too much spending on the arms race and the war.
- There had been almost no new thinking about how to run the Soviet economy since the days of Stalin. Each leader had followed the same policies and had ignored the warning signs that things were going wrong.
- Brezhnev had reverted to Stalin's policy of repression. There was little or no constructive reform.

Gorbachev and changing attitudes

In March 1985, Mikhail Gorbachev became leader of the USSR and immediately set about reforming the old Soviet system. He started to improve relations with the USA, developing very good relations with President Reagan.

Gorbachev and international policy

- Gorbachev realised that the USSR could not afford an arms race with the USA.
- He accepted President Reagan's invitation to meet with him in Geneva in November 1985.
- In 1987, after several meetings, Gorbachev and Reagan signed the Intermediate-range Nuclear Forces (INF) treaty, which removed all medium-range nuclear weapons from Europe.
- SALT (see page 56) had developed into START (Strategic Arms Reduction Talks) and, on an official visit to Washington in December 1988, Gorbachev also proposed deep cuts in conventional (non-nuclear) American and Soviet forces.

Key term

Satellite state: a country under the influence or control of another state.

Exam practice

1 Which was the more important reason for worsening relations between the USA and the USSR in the years 1979–84?
   - the Soviet invasion of Afghanistan
   - the policies of Ronald Reagan

   You must refer to **both** reasons in your answer.   *(10 marks)*

Exam tip
Exam practice question 1 above is a Unit 1 question. Ensure you refer to both reasons in your answer and come to a judgement. You could decide that both reasons were of equal importance – but explain why.

Perestroika and *glasnost*

Gorbachev was the decisive figure in this period. He firmly believed that the USSR could not continue to compete with the USA and that the Soviet Union needed to be reformed. The twin themes of his policies were:

- *perestroika* – changing some economic policies to allow more competition and more incentives to produce goods. Gorbachev wanted to change the government-controlled economy in place since the time of Stalin
- *glasnost* – openness in government. Gorbachev thought people should be allowed, within reason, to say what they believe with more open debate.

Some Communists criticised Gorbachev for allowing these freedoms. In some respects, their criticisms were valid. Once Gorbachev allowed freedom of speech, he could not control what was said or written in the media. Whereas Gorbachev wanted reforms within Communism, some wanted to get rid of Communism altogether. This sentiment was even stronger in the countries of eastern Europe.

The end of Soviet control in eastern Europe

During 1989, Gorbachev was at the height of his international popularity. He met the new American president, George Bush, and together they announced the end of the Cold War. In 1990, Gorbachev was awarded the Nobel Peace Prize. Yet in 1989, Soviet control of eastern Europe was collapsing rapidly.

The Communist countries of eastern Europe had become increasingly discontented during the 1980s. It gradually became clear that the Soviet Union had neither the will nor the power to put down demonstrations or prevent changes in these nations' systems of government. Even so, the speed of the collapse of Soviet control amazed everyone.

- Poland: free elections were held in June 1989. Lech Walesa became the first non-Communist leader in eastern Europe since 1945.
- East Germany: the unpopular East German leader, Erich Honecker, tried to prevent change, but his troops refused to fire on the demonstrators. In November 1989 the Berlin Wall was pulled down.
- Czechoslovakia: in November 1989 there were huge anti-Communist demonstrations. Vaclav Havel, a popular playwright, became the new leader of the country, with free elections in 1990.
- Romania: in a short and bloody revolution in December 1989, the unpopular Communist dictator, Nicolae Ceauşescu, and his wife Elena were shot.
- Bulgaria: the Communist leader resigned in November 1989 and free elections were held in 1990.
- The Baltic states: in 1990, Lithuania, Latvia and Estonia declared themselves independent of the Soviet Union.

> ## Comment
>
> *These new policies led to many practical changes within the USSR. Some political prisoners were released – for example, Andrei Sakharov, a nuclear physicist-turned-human rights campaigner, was allowed to return from exile. In 1987, changes in economic policy meant that people were allowed to buy and sell at a profit for the first time since the 1920s.*

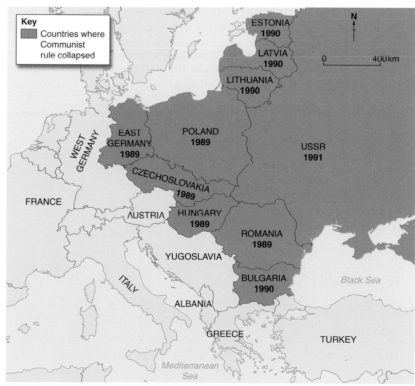

The collapse of Communism in eastern Europe.

The fall of the Berlin Wall

The fall of the Berlin Wall has come to symbolise the end of the Cold War. On 9 November 1989, the East German Government announced much greater freedom of travel for East German citizens, including crossing the border into West Germany. Thousands of East Berliners flocked to the checkpoints in the Berlin Wall and the border guards let them pass. Soon, the East Berliners were chipping away at and dismantling the Wall.

The collapse of the USSR

Gorbachev was seen as weak by many within the USSR. His promised reforms had not brought about improved living standards and he appeared to have simply accepted the collapse of Soviet influence in eastern Europe. Some in the USSR itself did not want the mere reform of Communism, but its abolition.

In February 1990, there was a huge demonstration in Moscow against the communist system. The various republics within the USSR increasingly demanded their freedom from the grip of the Union. The new President of the Russian republic, Boris Yeltsin, encouraged this process of breaking up the Soviet Union, and, in December 1991, he formally ended the Soviet Union. He also disbanded the Communist Party. Gorbachev resigned as Soviet President, as there was no longer a Soviet state for him to control.

There were, of course, huge implications for world affairs. In 1991, East and West Berlin were reunited, and East and West Germany became a single country. In other ex-Communist countries, there were less happy endings. For example, in Yugoslavia the Serbs refused to accept a Croat as leader, and Slovenia and Croatia declared independence in 1991, leading to a bloody civil war.

The era of Communism in eastern Europe was over.

SOURCE 1

Extract from the *Independent*, a national British newspaper, November 1989.

For most west Europeans now alive, the world has always ended at the East German border and the Wall. Beyond lay darkness. The pulling down of the Wall and the opening of the frontiers declares that the world has no edge any more. Europe is becoming once more round and whole.

Revision tasks

1 Draw a mind map to explain briefly the part played by the following in the collapse of the USSR:
   - *perestroika*
   - *glasnost*
   - Boris Yeltsin.

2 Why was Gorbachev so liked and so hated at the same time?

3 Make a copy of the table below. Summarise the key developments in each country in the years 1989–90.

	Key developments 1989–90
Poland	
Czechoslovakia	
East Germany	
Romania	
Bulgaria	
The Baltic states	

Exam practice

1 **Source 1** suggests possible consequences of Gorbachev's changes. Do you agree that these were the main consequences? Explain your answer by referring to:
   - the purpose of the source – what is it trying to make you believe?
   - its content – what is it suggesting about the consequences of Gorbachev's policies?
   - your own contextual knowledge – in other words, what do you know about the consequences of Gorbachev's policies? *(6 marks)*

6.2 What problems faced the USA and the UN following the end of the Cold War?

The role of the USA changed in the 1990s as a result of the end of the Cold War and the rivalry with the USSR.

The role of the USA in the Post-Cold War World

During the 1990s, American foreign policy focused on consolidating its success. The USA, because of its economic and military strength, became the only global superpower as well as the champion of democracy in the world. Together with its European allies, the USA set out to create, for the first time in history, a peaceful, undivided and democratic Europe based round the European Union.

- It continued to support NATO, originally set up to defend western Europe against Soviet expansion. Membership expanded to include eastern European states such as Poland, Hungary and the Czech Republic.
- NATO was seen by the USA as a means of maintaining the security of Europe as well as assisting with the changes in eastern Europe and the Balkans after the fall of Communism.
- Throughout the 1990s, NATO was used by the Americans in the Balkans to try to end the bouts of ethnic cleansing in Bosnia and Kosovo, part of the former Yugoslavia. In 1995, President Clinton worked with President Yeltsin of Russia to try to bring an end to the war in Bosnia, the outcome being the Dayton Accords. These agreements brought the three and a half year Bosnian War to an end, and provided a framework for peace and stability in the area.

Case studies of UN action in the 1990s

The USA also worked with the United Nations (UN) to resolve crises and enjoyed some success with Kuwait and Kosovo.

Kuwait

On 2 August 1990 Saddam Hussein, the ruler of Iraq, ordered the invasion of Kuwait, one of the leading oil-producing countries in the Middle East. In less than 24 hours, the country was under Iraqi control. Burdened with debts from his war with Iran, Kuwait offered a rich prize. Saddam did not expect the USA to use its military power in support of Kuwait. After all, the USA had been supporting him all the way through the war with the Iranian regime.

President Bush Snr took the lead in pressing for action to remove the Iraqis from Kuwait. He used the argument that it was an act of blatant aggression against a smaller neighbouring country. In reality, Bush wanted to protect US economic (especially oil) interests in the area.

The UN acted at once. The Security Council condemned the invasion and demanded withdrawal. On 6 August 1991, it passed Resolution 661, imposing economic sanctions on Iraq. This was followed by a period of diplomacy, but Saddam refused to withdraw. In November 1990, UN Resolution 678 authorised military action against Iraq if it failed to withdraw by 15 January 1991.

The USA organised a coalition of 34 nations with an armed force of 500,000. With almost 2,000 aircraft, General Norman Schwarzkopf, the US commander of the Coalition forces in the Gulf, opened with an air assault. Operation Desert Storm, the air offensive against Iraq, was launched on 16 January 1991. In the first ten hours, a combination of Stealth aircraft, cruise missiles, electronic warfare and precision-guided munitions took apart Iraq's military infrastructure and wrecked their ground forces.

After more than a month of 'softening up', Operation Desert Saber, the ground offensive to liberate Kuwait, was launched on 23 February. By 27 February, Kuwait City was taken by Coalition troops and the following day the US ordered a ceasefire. Saddam was allowed to withdraw with much of his army intact. Bush called a ceasefire because he was afraid that if the slaughter continued the allies would lose the support of the other Arab nations. It was widely expected outside Iraq that after his humiliating defeat, Saddam Hussein would soon be overthrown.

This was a success for the UN because:

- UN weapons inspectors were allowed into Iraq to make sure that he did not pose a threat to peace again.
- It had successfully used diplomatic, economic and military means, raising a powerful military force, to repel an aggressor.
- It had achieved all this by securing agreement among wider nations, thus avoiding any wider conflict.

However, Saddam Hussein was still leader of Iraq and remained a threat in the Middle East. In 2003, Coalition forces invaded Iraq and removed Saddam as leader.

Kosovo

Kosovo, a province between Albania and Serbia, was part of the Yugoslav federation. In 1974, it was given greater autonomy within the federation but, in the 1980s, it campaigned for full independence. On becoming president of the Yugoslav federation in 1989, Slobodan Milosevic, who was a champion of Serbian nationalism, proceeded to strip Kosovo of its autonomy. Two years later, leaders of Kosovo declared unilateral independence and, in the mid 1990s, an Albanian guerrilla movement, the Kosovo Liberation Army (KLA), stepped up attacks on Serb targets. The attacks precipitated a major Yugoslav military crackdown.

By the summer of 1998, Kosovo Albanians were mounting mass protests against Serbian rule and police and army reinforcements were sent in to crush the KLA.

This led to UN intervention. On 23 September 1998, the UN Security Council adopted Resolution 1199. This:

- expressed 'grave concern' at reports reaching the Secretary General that over 230,000 persons had been displaced from their homes by the actions of Serbian security forces and the Yugoslav Army;
- demanded that all parties in Kosovo and the Federal Republic of Yugoslavia (Serbia and Montenegro) cease hostilities and maintain a ceasefire.

Slobodan Milosevic's rejection of the UN resolution and other international attempts to end the persecution in Kosovo led to NATO air strikes against targets in Kosovo and Serbia in March 1999. However, a campaign of **ethnic cleansing** against Kosovo Albanians was launched by the Serbian authorities. Hundreds of thousands of refugees fled to Albania, Macedonia and Montenegro and further afield, and thousands died in the conflict. Serbian forces were driven out in the summer of 1999 and the UN took over the administration of the province.

Kosovo was a partial success for the UN:

- It had initially attempted a diplomatic solution.
- When this failed, it had used military intervention to force out the Serbian forces and end the ethnic cleansing.
- It had taken over the temporary administration of the province.

However, it was not a total success. The UN had not been able to prevent atrocities being carried out in Kosovo by Milosevic.

Key term

Ethnic cleansing: the systematic elimination of an ethnic group or groups from a region or society, as by deportation, forced emigration, or genocide.

Comment

Later in 1999, investigations by the Organisation for Security and Co-operation in Europe found that Serbs had carried out human rights abuses on a massive scale. Milosevic was put on trial in early 2002 at the International Criminal Tribunal for the former Yugoslavia in The Hague on charges of genocide and crimes against humanity. Milosevic died in 2006 and, later, the court was unable to establish legally what had actually happened in Kosovo. Ethnic Albanians were angry that Milosevic's death robbed them of a verdict.

Revision tasks

1 After the Cold War, in what ways did US policy in Europe:
   a) change
   b) stay the same?

2 Make a copy of the table below. Summarise the key features of UN involvement in Kuwait and Kosovo. In the last column, make a judgement about how successful the UN was in each crisis on a scale of 1–5 with 5 being totally successful. Give a brief explanation for each decision.

Crises	Causes	Events	Results	How successful (1–5)
Kuwait				
Kosovo				

Key content

You need to have a good working knowledge of the following areas.
Tick off each item once you are confident in your knowledge.

- ❏ Reagan and the renewal of the Cold War, especially SDI
- ❏ The reasons for and importance of Solidarity in Poland
- ❏ The economic and political effects of the Afghan war
- ❏ Gorbachev and co-operation with Reagan
- ❏ The policies of *perestroika* and *glasnost*
- ❏ The collapse of the USSR
- ❏ The end of Soviet control in eastern Europe
- ❏ US foreign policy in the 1990s
- ❏ UN intervention in Kuwait
- ❏ UN intervention in Kosovo

Check your knowledge online with our Quick quizzes at www.hodderplus.co.uk/modernworldhistory.

In 1914, Russia was ruled by Tsar Nicholas II and went to war against Germany and Austria. The war was a disaster, with defeat after defeat and economic, political and military chaos. In 1917, there were two revolutions, the first getting rid of the Tsar, the second creating a Communist government. After 1917, Lenin began the development of the first Communist country, during which there was also a civil war. Much had been achieved by the time of Lenin's death in 1924.

Key issues

As with all examination topics, you will be expected to do more than simply learn the content and write it out again. You will need to show understanding of key issues from the period. These are:

- Why did the rule of the Tsar collapse in February/March 1917?
- Why were the Bolsheviks able to seize power in October/ November 1917?
- How successful was Lenin in creating a new society in Russia?

7.1 Why did the rule of the Tsar collapse in February/March 1917?

The government of Nicholas II in 1914

The Russian monarch was known as the Tsar. He ruled as an **autocrat**. He believed that God had made him Tsar and that he therefore had absolute authority to rule Russia. The Tsar ruled with the support of the aristocracy (landowners), the Church, the army and the civil service.

Most tsars ruled harshly and crushed any opposition. Newspapers were censored and the Tsar used his secret police, the **Okhrana**, to track down anyone who was critical of his rule.

Nicholas II had become Tsar in 1894. He was very happily married to Alexandra, a German princess, and they had five children – four girls and a boy called Alexis. However, Nicholas was not well suited to ruling. He was weak and slow in making decisions, but determined to maintain his autocracy.

The nature of Russian society in 1914

Russia was a huge country with a population of nearly 150 million, spread across parts of Europe and Asia. Communications were poor, and most people did not travel much beyond their immediate neighbourhood.

The Russian economy was developing quickly in the years before 1914, especially in the period 1908–11. Russia, however, was still far behind modern industrial powers such as Britain, Germany and the USA. There was also much discontent.

> ### Key terms
>
> **Autocrat:** a ruler who holds absolute power in a country and does not have to explain his actions to anyone else.
> **Okhrana:** the secret police force of the Russian Tsars.

- The numbers working in industry were growing fast. Between 1880 and 1900, the population of Moscow doubled. As more and more people swarmed into the big cities, working and living conditions deteriorated rapidly. Food shortages, poor wages and terrible living conditions were commonplace.
- More than 80 per cent of the population were peasants living in the countryside on the estates of wealthy landlords. Most were unable to read or write and used outdated farming methods, which produced barely enough to live on.
- There was a significant minority of subject nationalities – Finns, Estonians, Poles, Latvians – who hated Russian rule and wanted independence.

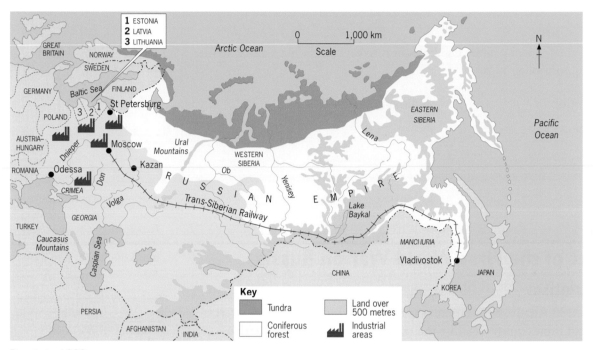

Russia in 1900.

The importance of traditional loyalties

Most Russian peasants were very loyal to the Tsar, even though they were very poor. They obeyed the priests who taught them that the Tsar was appointed by God. Thus society appeared to be very stable, even though **hierarchical** in structure.

The emergence of opposition groups

The Socialist Revolutionaries (SRs)

The SRs were the largest and most violent of the opposition groups, and were supported by many peasants.

- They wanted to carve up the huge estates of the nobility and hand them over to the peasants.
- They believed in violent struggle and were responsible for the assassination of two government officials as well as the murder of a great number of the Okhrana, or secret police.

The Social Democratic Party

This was a smaller party that followed the ideas of Karl Marx and Communism. The Communist state would be achieved through revolution by the proletariat (urban workers).

In 1903, the Social Democratic Party split into:

- Bolsheviks – led by Lenin, who believed it was the job of the party to create a revolution
- Mensheviks – who believed Russia was not ready for revolution.

> **Key term**
>
> **Hierarchical:** a society in which people are rigidly graded in order from the top (the Tsar and nobility) to the bottom (peasants).

Both the Socialist Revolutionaries and the Social Democratic Party were illegal, and many of their members were executed or sent into exile in Siberia.

Moderate opposition

Moderates did not want revolution. They included the Constitutional Democrats, or Kadets, set up in 1905 and led by Paul Miliukov. They were mostly lawyers, teachers, doctors and civil servants. They believed in working within the constitution, or laws, of Russia to bring about change, especially through the **Duma**.

Key term

Duma: a representative assembly that the Tsar consulted, but which had little power.

> ### Revision task
>
> Make a copy of the following table. Use key words to explain the aims and activities of the various opposition groups.
>
> | Opposition group | Aims/activities |
> |---|---|
> | Socialist Revolutionaries | |
> | Bolsheviks | |
> | Mensheviks | |
> | Kadets | |

Exam practice

1 Explain the reasons why there was opposition to Tsar Nicholas II in 1914.

(6 marks)

Exam tip For Exam practice question 1 above, you should aim to explain two or three causes (with some details) in order to reach the top level in the mark scheme.

The impact of the First World War on Russia

1. Initial patriotism

When war started in August 1914, there was much **patriotism**. Russians were fighting to defend their country against the invading Germans and Austrians. Priests prayed for success in the war.

Key term

Patriotism: proudly supporting one's country.

2. Military defeats

Continued military defeats increased the unpopularity of the Tsar. The Russian soldiers were poorly equipped due to shortages of weapons and ammunition. They suffered a series of crushing defeats at the hands of the Germans, including the Battle of Tannenburg in August 1914. The Brusilov offensive of 1916 was a great victory, but the Russians failed to take advantage of it and it was won at a high cost in terms of men and equipment. The Tsar took personal command of the army in 1915. This was a mistake as he was then directly to blame for any defeats.

3. Effects on the cities

There were major consequences for those living in towns and cities. These included:
- even greater overcrowding, accompanied by low wages and rapidly rising prices
- shortages of food and fuel. Many people were near starvation, especially in the winter. The winter of 1916–17 was extremely severe, even by Russian standards.

4. Transport dislocation

With vast distances to be covered, the transport system could not cope because:
- Priority was given to getting war materials and food to the troops on the frontline.
- Many locomotives and trucks were not repaired. Most skilled engineers had gone to fight in the war – and many of them had been killed. Sometimes food, intended for the cities, was left rotting in railway sidings.

The growing unpopularity of the Romanovs

As defeat and loss of life mounted, Nicholas II became more and more unpopular. This was especially true after he had taken personal command of the army in 1915. It meant that he was away from the capital city, Petrograd, for long periods, leaving his wife, Alexandra, in charge. However, as a German princess she was treated with suspicion by Russians, who were convinced that she was a German spy.

The role of Rasputin

Many of the Tsar's supporters were alarmed by the influence of the monk Rasputin over Nicholas and Alexandra. Rasputin seemed to be able to control the internal bleeding of their son, Alexis, who suffered from **haemophilia**. Several times he appeared to be near death when Rasputin 'cured' him.

Rasputin became unpopular because of his womanising, drinking and coarse habits. Often, in the absence of the Tsar, he influenced Alexandra in making decisions. Several capable ministers were dismissed and friends of Rasputin appointed in their place. Although he was killed by a group of nobles in December 1916, the damage to the reputation of the Tsar and his government had already been inflicted.

The Tsar's abdication, March 1917

Major unrest began in February 1917 with a strike by 40,000 workers at the Putilov armaments works in Petrograd. Discontent and strikes in the city spread quickly. Long queues for food turned into bread riots. The Tsar was away with the fighting armies. When he ordered the troops to put down the riots, increasingly the soldiers refused to obey orders. The workers began to form councils (called soviets).

When the Tsar tried to return to Petrograd, his train was stopped and put in a siding. He was persuaded by Russian army commanders to abdicate because it was the best way to stop bloodshed and restore order. Meanwhile, the leaders of the Duma reluctantly took control of the Government.

> ### Comment
> *The capital city, St Petersburg, was renamed Petrograd at the beginning of the war. It was thought that the original name was too German-sounding.*

> ### Key term
> **Haemophilia:** a condition in which the blood fails to clot, leading to extensive internal bleeding.

> **Exam tip** Details of the death of Rasputin are interesting, but they are not likely to be relevant in an exam answer!

> ### Comment
> *Russia used the old Julian calendar, which was thirteen days behind the calendar used in western Europe. Using the Julian calendar, the events leading up to the revolution happened in February, with the Tsar's abdication on 2 March. According to the western calendar, he abdicated on 15 March.*

Revision tasks

1 Write your own definitions of the following terms:
   - autocracy
   - Duma
   - Okhrana
   - patriotism.

   To check your understanding, compare your answers with the definitions given in this book.

2 How did the following groups disagree with the way in which the Tsar ruled? Draw up a table like the one below to summarise the differences.

	Disagreement with the Tsar's rule
Kadets	
SRs	
Mensheviks	
Bolsheviks	

3 Using one of the following methods, summarise the main events leading to the abdication of the Tsar in March 1917:
   - a flow chart
   - a story board
   - a cartoon strip.

7.2 Why were the Bolsheviks able to seize power in October/November 1917?

The problems facing the Provisional Government

The Duma leaders set up what became known as the Provisional Government – 'provisional' because it was intended to be temporary until proper elections could be held. It faced many problems that were not easy to solve.

- Sharing power with the soviets – the soviets only carried out the orders of the Provisional Government if they agreed with them. Hostility from the Petrograd Soviet (workers' council) became worse as the Government failed to deal with economic and social problems.
- The inherited economic situation – food shortages, high prices, transport problems, low wages and poor working conditions all remained.
- Peasants and the land – the peasants were simply taking over the landowners' estates, while the Provisional Government failed to make a decision about the future of land ownership. It was said that this important reform should wait for a new government chosen by the people.
- The revolutionary parties began to thrive with less censorship – for example, any political views could be published. Political prisoners were released from prisons. In this more open situation, the Petrograd Soviet worked for political change.
- The war – the Provisional Government honoured Russia's commitments to its allies, but this led to more defeats and more discontent. Failure to end the war worsened the problems in the cities.

The failures of the Provisional Government

The Provisional Government failed to solve the main problems it faced. In June, its first Prime Minister, Prince Lvov, was replaced by the young lawyer, Alexander Kerensky. Meanwhile, the revolutionary parties continued to exist openly. Lenin, the Bolshevik leader, returned from Germany to Russia. He announced his 'April Theses'. These outlined how the Bolsheviks would overthrow the Provisional Government. However, his famous slogans such as 'Peace, Bread and Land' and 'All power to the soviets' began to get the Bolsheviks more attention in the main cities such as Petrograd.

The Provisional Government tried to gain support and restore morale by waging an offensive against Germany and Austria. It was hoped that this would lead to military victories. Instead the offensive in June 1917 led to defeats, further German advances and more desertions from the Russian armed forces.

The Provisional Government had to deal with an attempt to overthrow it in September 1917. This was led by General Kornilov, Commander-in-Chief of the army. His plan to restore strong government appealed to many of the middle and upper classes. Kornilov led a march on Petrograd which was stopped by the Bolsheviks, who were loaned weapons to do so by the Provisional Government.

> **Comment**
>
> *Lenin's return to Russia was assisted by the Germans. They hoped that Lenin would cause more trouble for the Provisional Government and so reduce its ability to fight against Germany.*

The growth of Bolshevik organisation in 1917

The Bolsheviks were greatly helped by the weakness of the Provisional Government. However, they contributed to their own growth in strength during the spring, summer and autumn of 1917.

- After the Tsar's abdication, Lenin returned to Russia determined to make use of the mass discontent caused by the First World War for the benefit of the Bolshevik Party. Lenin had devoted his life in preparation for such an opportunity.

- In May 1917, a Bolshevik Party Congress committed the Bolsheviks to claiming all power for the soviets – that is, a takeover of the Government by the workers. A half-hearted attempt in July (which failed) made the Bolsheviks look weaker, but Lenin had learned what was needed for a successful takeover.
- The defeat of General Kornilov in September 1917 was achieved mainly by the Bolsheviks. They were seen as heroes, saving Russia from military rule.
- By September, the Bolsheviks were the largest party in the Petrograd Soviet.
- Trotsky, who had joined the Bolsheviks in summer 1917, became chairman of the Military Revolutionary Committee, which planned a takeover on behalf of the Petrograd Soviet.

Revision tasks

1 Draw up a table listing the problems faced by the Provisional Government. For each problem, describe how far it was tackled or solved.

2 List the strengths and weaknesses of the Bolsheviks in summer 1917.

Bolshevik seizure of power, October/November 1917

In October 1917, Lenin was convinced that the time was right to overthrow the Provisional Government. Trotsky was put in charge of military planning. The Provisional Government under Kerensky knew that something was being planned but was powerless to stop it.

- **Night of 6 November** – Bolsheviks gained control of the Peter and Paul Fortress, main bridges, railway stations, banks, telephone exchanges and power stations in and around Petrograd.
- **Night of 7 November** – a cruise ship under Bolshevik control, the *Aurora*, fired shots from the River Neva towards the Winter Palace where the Provisional Government was based. Members of the Red Guard attacked the palace and found little opposition as it was only being defended by some trainee cadets and a women's battalion.
- **Early on 8 November** – Lenin announced that the Bolsheviks had taken over the Government of Russia. Within a week, the Bolsheviks also controlled Moscow.

Reasons for Bolshevik success

Later, Bolshevik propaganda claimed that the Bolshevik takeover was a popular revolution and that the Red Guards succeeded against strong opposition. In fact, the Bolsheviks did not have the support of the majority of the Russian population. The Red Guards faced little opposition in either Petrograd or Moscow because most people in these two cities took little notice of what was happening.

Bolshevik success was due to other reasons.

- The Provisional Government was very unpopular. Few rallied to support Kerensky and there were no massive demonstrations demanding his return.
- Lenin played an important role. He had spent many years organising a disciplined party dedicated to revolution. His campaigning of 1917, especially his slogan 'Peace, Bread and Land', brought more support. By October, the Bolshevik Party had 800,000 members with supporters in strategic places. At least half the army supported them, as did the sailors at the important naval base at Kronstadt near Petrograd (see page 75). The major industrial centres, and the Petrograd and Moscow Soviets, were also pro-Bolshevik.
- The Bolshevik revolution is often described as a classic work of planning by Trotsky. He organised the seizure of key buildings and positions in the two major cities.

> ## Comment
> *The calendar again! The Bolsheviks seized power on 6 and 7 November according to the western calendar, but it was still October in Russia – and hence this revolution is popularly known as the October Revolution.*

> **Exam tip** Make sure that you do not get the events of the two revolutions in 1917 confused!

Revision tasks

Using the information on pages 70–72, answer the following questions.

1 Explain which groups of people were likely to support the following and why:
   ● the Provisional Government   ● the Bolsheviks.

2 Draw up a table like the one below to look at the reasons for the success of the Bolshevik revolution. Use key words to explain each reason. In the last column, rate the importance of each factor on a scale of 1–5, with 5 as the most important. Provide a key word explanation of your rating.

Reason	Explanation	Rating
Unpopularity of Provisional Government		
Kornilov revolt		
Work of Lenin		
Organisation of Trotsky		

3 Use one of the following methods to summarise the main events and situations leading to the Bolshevik takeover in Petrograd in October/November 1917:
   ● a flow chart   ● a story board   ● a cartoon strip.

Exam practice

1 Explain how the Bolsheviks were able to seize power in October/November 1917.   *(6 marks)*

Exam tip For Exam practice question 1 above, you should aim to explain two or three factors (with some details) in order to reach the top level in the mark scheme.

7.3 How successful was Lenin in creating a new society in Russia?

The initial establishment of totalitarian rule by the Bolsheviks

The Provisional Government was replaced by the Council of the People's Commissars under Lenin. Lenin's aims were clear. He followed the theories of the political thinker Karl Marx and wanted a 'dictatorship of the proletariat'.

This meant that the Bolshevik Party would govern Russia for the good of the workers and peasants. Lenin was not interested in democracy. The elections that were held in late 1917 showed that the Bolsheviks did not have the support of most Russians.

● The Constituent Assembly, which met in January 1918, contained twice as many Socialist Revolutionaries as Bolsheviks, and the SRs opposed Lenin.
● Bolshevik Red Guards closed down the Assembly. By July 1918, the Russian Congress of Soviets had agreed a new system of government for Russia.

The result was that Lenin effectively became a dictator, and his secret police (the Cheka) began to intimidate, imprison and murder political opponents.

The question of land was vitally important in Russia as farming was still by far the most important business. Lenin abolished the private ownership of land. This effectively meant that the peasants stripped lands from landowners and the Church. In reality, the countryside was in a state of chaos in the early Bolshevik days, and no government was truly in control. Bolshevik control was strong in the towns and cities but not in the countryside.

● There were soon food shortages because Russian money was worthless and the peasants were not being paid for their produce.
● Peasants did not trust the Bolsheviks, who wanted to reorganise farming from individual to collective (or co-operative) farming.

The end of the First World War for Russia

The Bolsheviks had always planned to pull out of the war with Germany. They agreed a ceasefire in December 1917. Trotsky was given the job of negotiating terms but his only real achievement was to hold up the Germans until March 1918, when the Bolsheviks were forced to sign the Treaty of Brest-Litovsk.

- Russia lost vast amounts of territory (see map below).
- Russia lost important coal and iron resources and about one-third of its population.
- Russia also had to pay 300 million gold roubles in compensation.

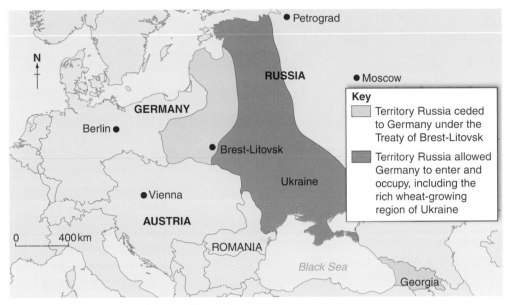

Russian losses under the Treaty of Brest-Litovsk.

Sources 1 and 2 give two viewpoints on Bolshevik rule during this period, and do not present a very favourable picture. However, Source 1 was written by an American during the Cold War. Such writings from the 1960s must be used with care as they may not be very reliable. Source 2 is from a historical novel. It is based on historical research and it fits many things you know from your background knowledge. When looking at sources such as these the skills of the historian must be used carefully to make a judgement.

Revision task

Which of **Sources 1** and **2** do you think is more useful for studying conditions in Russia in the first few months of Communist rule? Draw up a table to compare the usefulness of the two sources.

The causes and nature of the Civil War, 1918–21

Who made up the opposition?

The Bolsheviks did not have the support of all Russians when they seized power. By May 1918, they had more enemies, especially after the losses of the Treaty of Brest-Litovsk. By the summer of 1918, the Bolsheviks were faced with a range of opponents united only by their opposition to the Bolsheviks. These opponents, called the Whites (in contrast to the Bolshevik Red Guards), were made up of former tsarists, Mensheviks, Socialist Revolutionaries and foreign powers opposed to the new regime in Russia.

SOURCE 1

Leonard Schapiro, *The Communist Party of the Soviet Union*, 1963.

Bolshevik practice within a few days of 25th October was at variance with Lenin's repeated promises that when they were in power the Bolsheviks would guarantee to each political party ... facilities for publishing a newspaper. Some socialist and liberal papers, as well as the conservative papers, were closed down in the first few days.

SOURCE 2

Eugenie Fraser, *The House by the Dvina*, a historical novel, 1984.

In the town, after six months of living under our new government, conditions remained chaotic. The minds of the authorities are too occupied with establishing their doctrine and persecuting those who have opinions contrary to their own, to bother with the less important matters such as clothing and feeding hungry citizens.

The Bolsheviks in danger

In the early stages of the Civil War, the Bolsheviks were facing several threats.

- The Czech legion (which was made up of former prisoners of war) had seized sections of the vital Trans-Siberian railway.
- Admiral Kolchak had set up a White government in Siberia and was marching on Moscow.
- General Denikin was advancing with his army from southern Russia.
- Northern Russia, led by General Yudenich, was opposing the Bolsheviks.
- There were also risings against the Bolsheviks in Ukraine and Turkestan.
- Foreign powers supplied the Whites with arms and weapons and later landed troops to help the Whites. American, Japanese, French and British troops landed at Archangel, Murmansk and Vladivostok.

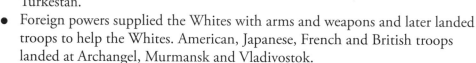

Key

Baltic states
1 Estonia
2 Latvia
3 Lithuania

General Denikin — White armies and their leaders

British — Foreign armies of intervention

Land under Bolshevik control, 1919

Bolshevik, White and foreign forces involved in the Civil War.

Bolshevik victory

Against what seemed to be overwhelming odds, the Bolsheviks won the Civil War. The crucial year was 1919. Under Trotsky's leadership, the Red Army defeated Kolchak and destroyed the Czech legion. Denikin's advance on Moscow was stopped and, by 1920, he was being pushed back. By late 1920, White forces were completely defeated. The Bolsheviks had won due to their ruthless, disciplined commitment and the failings of their enemies.

The strengths of the Bolsheviks were:

- They had large, well-organised armies under Trotsky, and good communication.
- They made good use of propaganda to show that the Whites were in league with foreigners and wanted to bring back the Tsar.
- Together with the Cheka (secret police), they kept a ruthless control over the Bolshevik territories, making sure that most people obeyed Lenin's rule.
- The Red Army was supplied by the brutal policy of 'War Communism' (see page 75), which ensured that troops and towns were fed and supplied.
- They held major towns with factories and industries to support the war effort.

The failings of the Whites were:

- They had no aim upon which they all agreed – in some cases, they disliked each other almost as much as they opposed the Reds.
- Their forces were spread across a huge area and they could not co-ordinate their attacks – they were beaten one by one.
- Their harsh treatment of people in the lands they captured led many to support the Bolsheviks against them.

The Civil War was a chaotic time in Russia's history. Many records were lost or destroyed at the time; some were doctored and many more are unreliable.

Look at Sources 3 and 4 on page 75, which provide evidence on the actions of the Whites in the Civil War. How useful are they in explaining why the Bolsheviks won the war?

Comment

It was at this time in July 1918 that all the members of the Russian royal family were massacred at Ekaterinburg by local Bolsheviks to prevent them falling into White hands.

Revision task

Make a table of comparisons between War Communism and the NEP.

War Communism	The NEP

SOURCE 3

From the memoirs of Colonel M.G. Drozdovsky, 1923.

The mounted platoon [of Whites] entered the village, met the Bolshevik committee and put the members to death ... Then the population was ordered to deliver without pay the best cattle, pigs ... and bread for the whole detachment.

SOURCE 4

Christopher Hill, *Lenin and the Russian Revolution*, 1947.

Not infrequently, the peasants said ... 'The Bolsheviks are rather unpleasant people, we do not like them, but still they are better than the White Guards.'

Exam practice

1 What does **Source 3** suggest about the methods used by the Whites in the Civil War? *(4 marks)*

The creation of the USSR

As various areas of the former Russian empire came under Bolshevik control, they were declared to be socialist republics. In December 1922, Lenin announced the existence of the USSR – the Union of Soviet Socialist Republics – but it only came into effect after Lenin's death in 1924.

Economic problems: War Communism and the New Economic Policy

War Communism

To defeat his opponents in the civil war, Lenin knew that he had to make sure that his armies were fed and equipped. To achieve this, he introduced in 1918 the policy of '**War Communism**'.

- Land and industry were 'nationalised' – taken over by the state.
- In the factories, there was severe discipline (for example, strikers could be shot) and key items, such as food and coal, were rationed.
- In the countryside, peasants were forced to hand over their surplus produce (what they did not need themselves) to the Government.
- Opposition was rooted out and destroyed by the Cheka (even the royal family was executed).

The cost of the civil war and War Communism

By 1921, Lenin was facing a shattered and demoralised country.

- War Communism had made the industrial workers poor and restless.
- War Communism and war damage had led to famine in the countryside – millions died in 1921.

The Kronstadt mutiny was a turning point. The Kronstadt sailors had been leading supporters of the revolution, but they revolted against War Communism in February 1921.

Although the Kronstadt revolt was put down by Trotsky and the civil war was being won, it was clear in 1921 that Lenin had to do something to improve people's living conditions. His solution was the New Economic Policy (NEP).

The New Economic Policy (NEP)

Lenin introduced the NEP at the Bolshevik Party Congress in March 1921. Its measures were simple but controversial.

- Peasants could keep part of their surpluses to sell at a profit.
- Small factories were given back to private ownership.
- Small private businesses could be set up to trade at a profit.

Some Communists saw the NEP as a betrayal, but Lenin saw it as a temporary measure to keep the Russian people happy and get the economy moving. All of the major industries remained in state hands, and political control (under the Cheka) remained very strict.

Exam tip
For Exam practice question 1 above you can get up to two marks for quoting relevant bits from the source. The other two marks are for making inferences or deductions – that is, finding things that the source is suggesting without being openly stated.
Be clear about some of the details of the Civil War. If you include some names (for example, of generals) in your answer this will impress the examiner.

Key term

War Communism: it had the *appearance* of Communism, but was carried out due to Bolshevik necessities during the civil war.

The roles and achievements of Lenin and Trotsky

The importance of Lenin

Lenin died in January 1924. He had brought about huge changes in Russia.

- He had led the Communist revolution.
- He had established the USSR (Union of Soviet Socialist Republics).
- He had created a powerful, disciplined Communist Party by using the Cheka to purge (remove) opponents of his policies.
- The USSR had become a one-party state, which was effectively a dictatorship, where the Communist Party controlled industry, the army, the police, the press – in fact, almost all aspects of life.

Lenin has often had a 'good press' in history, especially when compared to his successor, Stalin. The questions that historians are now asking are: What kind of man was Lenin? Was he as ruthless as Stalin? Was he good for Russia?

Sources 5 and 6 present two differing views from British newspapers immediately after the death of Lenin. For historians, these are useful sources – they show the attitudes of the day very clearly. *The Times* was a conservative newspaper that opposed Socialism and Communism. It shows what many of its conservative readers would think of Lenin. The *Daily Herald* was also a British newspaper, but was more favourable towards Socialism and Communism. Again, its comments reveal what many of its readers probably thought about Lenin. However, neither source is reliable for telling us what Lenin was actually like. They each express only an opinion. We cannot therefore simply accept what they say as true without question.

The importance of Trotsky

Trotsky also played an important role in the period 1917–24.

- He organised the Red Guards in Petrograd in 1917 in his role of chairman of the Military Revolutionary Committee.
- He planned and organised the Bolshevik takeover in autumn 1917.
- He recruited, trained and led the Red Army during the Civil War of 1918–21.
- He was responsible for the Red Terror during the Civil War, which discouraged Russians from supporting the Whites.
- He was clearly the most important Bolshevik under Lenin.

Key content

You need to have a good working knowledge of the following areas.
Tick off each item once you are confident in your knowledge.

- ❏ Government and society in Russia in 1914
- ❏ The emergence of opposition groups
- ❏ Initial patriotism at the beginning of the First World War
- ❏ The effects of military defeats; economic and social consequences of the war
- ❏ The reasons for the Tsar's abdication and Rasputin's role
- ❏ The problems faced by the Provisional Government
- ❏ The growing unpopularity of the Provisional Government
- ❏ The growth of support for Bolsheviks and their seizure of power
- ❏ Initial Bolshevik policies, including the Treaty of Brest-Litovsk
- ❏ The Civil War: causes, nature and reasons for Bolshevik success; the consequences
- ❏ War Communism and the New Economic Policy
- ❏ The roles and achievements of Lenin and Trotsky

Check your knowledge online with our Quick quizzes at www.hodderplus.co.uk/modernworldhistory.

SOURCE 5

The Times, 23 January 1924

This extraordinary man was first and foremost a professional revolutionary … A man of iron will and inflexible ambition, he was absolutely ruthless and used human beings as mere material for his purpose.

SOURCE 6

Daily Herald, 23 January 1924

Lenin is dead. All through Russia that news has struck as a deep personal loss. For 'Ilyitch' was loved of his own Russian people – whom he understood and loved so well – as no leader of men in our time has been loved.

Exam practice

1 Study **Source 5** OR **Source 6**. How useful is this source for studying the achievements of Lenin? Use the source and your knowledge to explain your answer. *(10 marks)*

Exam tip For Exam practice question 1 above you should aim to write two paragraphs. One should be trying to assess how useful the source is likely to be, bearing in mind its likely purpose. The other should be about the content of the source – is it accurate? In both paragraphs you should provide some detailed explanation for a high mark.

In November 1918, Germany surrendered to the Allies at the end of the First World War. The country was in chaos and there were attempts at revolution by both right- and left-wing groups. There were economic problems as well, including hyperinflation, and the German economy appeared to be in ruins. After 1923, Germany appeared to recover well under Stresemann's guidance and, for many, prosperity and optimism returned. However, all this ended with the Wall Street Crash in the autumn of 1929, opening the way for extremists such as Hitler.

Key issues

As with all examination topics, you will be expected to do more than simply learn the content and write it out again. You will need to show understanding of key issues from the period. These are:

● How far do the early problems of the Weimar Republic suggest that it was doomed from the start?
● How far did the Weimar Republic recover under Stresemann?
● How far did the Nazi Party develop its ideas and organisation up to 1929?

8.1 How far do the early problems of the Weimar Republic suggest that it was doomed from the start?

The origins of the Weimar Republic

When it became apparent that Germany was losing the First World War, the German **Kaiser**, Wilhelm II, abdicated. In November 1918, the Government of Germany was left in the hands of the **Chancellor**, Friedrich Ebert. He gave the orders for the **armistice** to be signed, which meant that the German armed forces surrendered. Meanwhile, Ebert and his colleagues drew up a new democratic **constitution** for Germany. In the summer of 1919, Ebert was elected as the first President of this new **Weimar Republic**.

The effects of the Treaty of Versailles

The Treaty of Versailles was very bad for Germany, both in terms of what the country lost, and the effect on people's attitudes to the new Government, even though Germany had no choice about signing the treaty.

● The new republic got off to a bad start and was immediately associated with the humiliating treaty.
● Opponents of the republic, especially the army, blamed the Government for signing the armistice that led to the treaty. They referred to the Government as

Key terms

Kaiser: emperor.
Chancellor: chief minister (equivalent of Prime Minister in Britain).
Armistice: a ceasefire.
Constitution: an agreed method of governing a country, with the details usually written down and agreed on by those being governed.
Weimar Republic: a republic is a country without a hereditary ruler, such as a king or emperor. The new Government first met in the town of Weimar.

the 'November Criminals', a reference to the signing of the armistice on 11 November.

- The Government was accused of having stabbed the German army in the back. In other words, the German army would have won the war if the armistice had not been signed. This, of course, was not true.
- Germany could not afford to pay the reparations. The country had been run down by the war and had lost important areas of land that could make money, such as the coalfields of the Saar.

Cross reference

For full details of the terms of the Treaty of Versailles and its effects on Germany, see Chapter 2, pages 19–21.

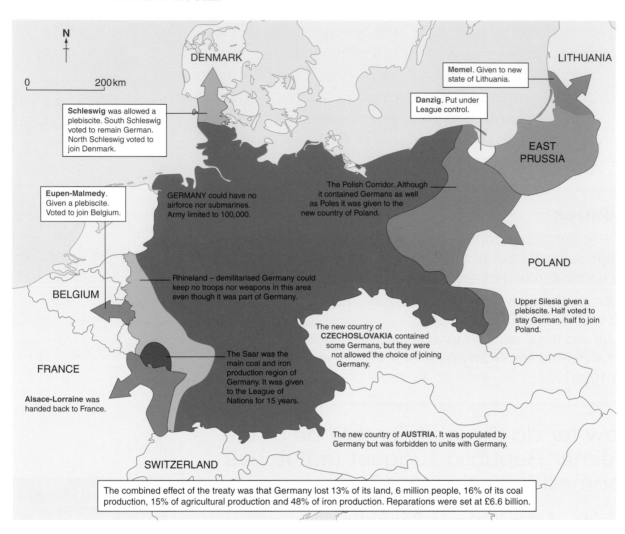

N

0   200km

Schleswig was allowed a plebiscite. South Schleswig voted to remain German. North Schleswig voted to join Denmark.

DENMARK

LITHUANIA

Memel. Given to new state of Lithuania.

Danzig. Put under League control.

EAST PRUSSIA

Eupen-Malmedy. Given a plebiscite. Voted to join Belgium.

GERMANY could have no airforce nor submarines. Army limited to 100,000.

The Polish Corridor. Although it contained Germans as well as Poles it was given to the new country of Poland.

POLAND

BELGIUM

Rhineland – demilitarised Germany could keep no troops nor weapons in this area even though it was part of Germany.

Upper Silesia given a plebiscite. Half voted to stay German, half to join Poland.

FRANCE

The Saar was the main coal and iron production region of Germany. It was given to the League of Nations for 15 years.

The new country of CZECHOSLOVAKIA contained some Germans, but they were not allowed the choice of joining Germany.

Alsace-Lorraine was handed back to France.

The new country of AUSTRIA. It was populated by Germany but was forbidden to unite with Germany.

SWITZERLAND

The combined effect of the treaty was that Germany lost 13% of its land, 6 million people, 16% of its coal production, 15% of agricultural production and 48% of iron production. Reparations were set at £6.6 billion.

The effect of the Treaty of Versailles on Germany.

Revision task

Using the map above and the details on the previous page, list the main reasons why most Germans hated the Treaty of Versailles. Divide the list into:

- military issues
- land issues
- blame for defeat.

The constitution of Weimar Germany

In theory, the new Weimar Constitution gave Germany a nearly perfect democratic system. The 'lower house', or Reichstag, was elected by **proportional representation**. The vote was by secret ballot and universal suffrage (everyone could vote). Elections were to be held at least every four years.

The 'upper house', or Reichsrat, was made up of representatives from each of the German states. It could delay new laws.

Key term

Proportional representation: a system in which the number of representatives from a given party is determined by how many votes that party gains nationally.

The President was also the head of state and was elected every seven years. The President appointed the Chancellor (usually the head of the largest party in the Reichstag) to form a government. The Chancellor's role was therefore similar to the Prime Minister's role in Britain.

Consequences of the Weimar instability

In practice, the new government and its problems led to worrying instability.

- In 1919, the republic had many enemies. Was it sensible to give equal rights to those who wished to destroy it?
- Proportional representation encouraged lots of small parties. It was difficult for one party to get a majority so governments had to be **coalitions** where two or more parties joined together. This led to weak governments.
- The President had too much power. Article 48 of the Constitution said that in an emergency, the President could abandon democracy and rule by decree. This proved disastrous in the period 1929–33.
- The generals in charge of the army were the same men who had fought the war for the Kaiser. Many of them opposed the republic and wanted the Kaiser to return.
- The judges in the new Germany were the same men who had served under the Kaiser. They had sympathy with those who were against the republic.

Challenges to the Weimar Government, 1919–23

1. The Spartacists – the main threat from the left wing

- Communists in Germany, known as Spartacists, wanted a revolution similar to that in Russia in 1917 (see page 69).
- In January 1919, Communist activists led by Karl Liebknecht and Rosa Luxemburg seized power in Berlin and the Baltic ports.
- In Bavaria, an independent socialist state was created under the leadership of Kurt Eisner.
- Within weeks, however, all the revolts had been crushed by regular troops and ex-soldiers (Freikorps). The Communist leaders were assassinated.

2. Attempted takeovers by the right wing

German **nationalists** thought democracy was weak. For many nationalists, the new Weimar Republic was a symbol of Germany's defeat in the war. They were furious with the Government for signing the Treaty of Versailles. They wanted to see a strong government that would make Germany great again.

- In March 1920, Wolfgang Kapp, an extreme nationalist, and a group of Freikorps units seized power in Berlin. This became known as the Kapp **Putsch**.
- Kapp was not supported by the workers in the factories. The workers organised a strike in Berlin in support of the Government. Within hours, the German capital came to a halt and supplies of gas, water and coal stopped.
- After four days, Kapp and his supporters gave up and fled Berlin. Ebert and the Weimar Government returned to power.

3. Political instability

With coalition governments and much violence, the Weimar Government was always struggling to maintain support. Riots and lawlessness were common, and two leading Weimar politicians were murdered.

- The German Finance Minister, Matthias Erzberger, was murdered by extreme nationalists. He had been the leading German representative at the signing of the peace treaty in Versailles in 1919.

Key terms

Coalition: the joining together of two or more political parties in a situation where no one political party gets a majority of the votes, in order to have sufficient support to pass laws.
Nationalists: those wanting a strong unified Germany, with a government that was similar to the one under the Kaiser before the war.
Putsch: an attempt to seize control and gain power by force.

- Four extreme nationalists shot the popular German Jewish Foreign Minister, Walther Rathenau. He had recently negotiated the Treaty of Rapallo to improve relations with Communist Russia. Many nationalists were fanatically anti-Communist and anti-Semitic.

This instability reached its peak in 1923 when Germany suffered an invasion of the Ruhr by the French, the consequences of hyperinflation, and an attempted takeover by Hitler and the Nazi Party, known as the Munich Putsch. (See pages 83–4 for details of the Munich Putsch.)

4. Reparations and the invasion of the Ruhr

According to the terms of the Treaty of Versailles, Germany had to pay for the damage caused during the First World War. These payments were known as reparations and were a major burden to the new state.

- The Reparations Commission announced that Germany would be required to pay £6,600 million in gold in annual instalments.
- In 1922, the German Government announced it would not be able to pay and asked for more time.

The British Government agreed to this but the French Government insisted that Germany must pay. In January 1923, the French and Belgian Governments sent troops into the Ruhr, the centre of German industry. The results were disastrous for Germany.

- German workers used **passive resistance** against the invaders.
- The German economy ground to a halt.

Key term

Passive resistance: a form of opposition in which people do not fight but refuse to co-operate.

5. Hyperinflation

The problem of making the reparation payments encouraged the Weimar Government to print more and more money. However, printing money simply caused prices to rise out of control and hyperinflation set in. The German mark became virtually worthless.

Value of the German mark against the US dollar, 1914–23	
1914	$1 = 4 marks
1922	$1 = 7,000 marks
July 1923	$1 = 160,000 marks
November 1923	$1 = 4,200,000,000 marks

- As prices rose, people's savings became worthless (this hit the middle classes particularly hard). In 1923, prices in shops were increased almost every hour.
- At times, workers were paid twice a day so that they might be able to buy food before prices rose again.
- People on fixed incomes (such as pensioners) suffered badly.
- Prices rose much faster than incomes and many people starved as they were unable to afford food or fuel.

Revision tasks

1 Use the information on pages 79–80 to complete the table below. Write a key word summary of each event and give each one a rating on a scale of 1 to 10 in terms of its seriousness for the Weimar Republic (10 is the most serious).

Threat	Date	Outline of events	Rating
Spartacist revolt			
Kapp Putsch			
French invasion of the Ruhr			
Hyperinflation			

2 Think through what you have studied about German history in the first years following the First World War. Did the Weimar Republic have a good chance of long-term success?

Start by drawing up a list of its problems, and then a list of the factors that might suggest it was capable of providing long-term stability for Germany.

Exam practice

1 Study Source 1 OR Source 2. How useful is this source for studying the role of the German Communists (the Spartacists) in 1918–19? *(10 marks)*

SOURCE 1

Rosa Luxemburg in late 1918.
The rule of the working class means real democracy. It means the use of power to get rid of the middle- and upper-class people. It means the smashing of the ruling classes with all the brutality that the working class can develop.

SOURCE 2

From an article in a German government newspaper, early January 1919.
The terrible actions of Liebknecht and Rosa Luxemburg spoil the revolution and threaten all its achievements. The masses must not sit quiet for one minute longer and allow these brutal beasts to force the people into civil war.

> **Exam tip** For Exam practice question 1 on the left you should aim to write two paragraphs. One should be trying to assess how useful the source is likely to be, bearing in mind its likely purpose. The other should be about the content of the source – is it accurate? In both paragraphs you should provide some detailed explanation for a high mark.

8.2 How far did the Weimar Republic recover under Stresemann?

The role of Stresemann

As Chancellor, Stresemann tried to stabilise Germany's financial position. Stresemann became Foreign Secretary in 1924 and was mainly responsible for the Dawes Plan and German success abroad. He died in October 1929, on the eve of the Wall Street Crash. He was one of the few Weimar politicians strong enough to appeal to the German people.

Stresemann and the economic crisis, 1923

In September 1923, at the height of the economic crisis, a new government was formed by Gustav Stresemann.
- He stopped the printing of worthless paper money in November 1923.
- He created a new currency called the Rentenmark.
- He also called off the resistance against the French occupation by German workers in the Ruhr. The German economy began to recover slowly, although French troops did not withdraw from the Ruhr until 1925.

The recovery of the economy

This was encouraged by the introduction of:
- the Rentenmark, which replaced the old worthless mark
- the Dawes Plan of 1924 – in return for Germany starting to pay reparations once more, the USA agreed to lend Germany 800 million marks. This could be used to build new factories to produce jobs and goods, and to raise people's standard of living.

During this period, the Weimar Republic seemed to recover from the problems of its early years. This is often referred to as the 'Golden Age' of the Republic. The success was due to several reasons.
- In 1925, the French and Belgian troops left the Ruhr.
- In 1929, the Young Plan was introduced, which reduced reparations by over 67 per cent.

- In 1928, industrial production finally improved on pre-First World War levels. By 1930, Germany was one of the leading exporters of manufactured goods.
- In nearly every town, new factories and public facilities sprang up. New roads, railways, and nearly 3 million homes were built.

However, unemployment was rising quite quickly in the later 1920s – a sign of future problems.

Developments in international relations

Stresemann, Foreign Secretary at this time, was responsible for several successes in foreign policy.
- In 1925, Germany signed the Locarno Treaties with Britain, France and Italy. These guaranteed Germany's frontiers with France and Belgium.
- In 1926, Stresemann took Germany into the League of Nations. Germany was recognised as a great power and was given a permanent seat on the League's Council alongside France and Britain.
- In 1928, Germany signed the Kellogg–Briand Pact along with 64 other nations. It was agreed that they would keep their armies for self-defence but 'the solution of all disputes shall only be sought by peaceful means'.

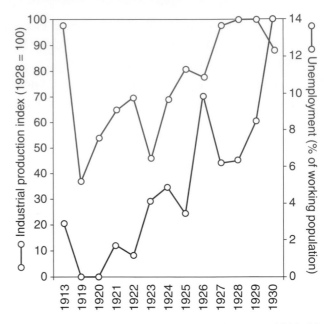

Changes in industrial output and unemployment, 1913–30.

The extent of recovery

The period 1924–29 saw more stable governments. After the 1928 election, the Social Democrats, for the first time since 1923, joined a government coalition with the other parties that supported the republic. This showed that the middle-class parties were no longer so suspicious of the socialists. There was less support for extreme parties such as the National Socialist German Workers' Party (the Nazis), who won only twelve seats in the Reichstag in the elections of 1928. The Communists also did less well in 1924 and 1928 compared with the earlier 1920s.

Economically, Germany was thriving. Hyperinflation had been overcome; reparation payments were being made; industries were expanding; the living standard of many Germans was improving.

There was also a flourishing of culture in Weimar Germany. With the free expression of ideas, writers, poets, artists and architects were at liberty to experiment. The most famous novel to come out of Weimar Germany, *All Quiet on the Western Front* by Erich Remarque, criticised war. In three months, it sold half a million copies. This was also a golden age for the German cinema. There were big advances in film-making technique with silent films and, at the end of the 1920s, films with sound, known as 'talkies' (talking pictures).

Berlin rivalled Paris as the cultural capital of Europe, but there was also a lot of decadence and corruption, centred around nightclubs and cabaret shows.

However, there were still serious problems.
- Germany depended on American loans, which could be withdrawn at any time.
- Farming suffered from depression throughout the 1920s due to a fall in food prices. Income from agriculture went down in the years 1925 to 1929.
- Extremist parties such as the Nazis and the Communists were determined to overthrow the Weimar Republic. In 1924, the Communists held 45 seats in the Reichstag and this grew to 54 seats in the 1928 election.
- In 1925, Hindenburg was elected President. He had been one of Germany's war leaders under the Kaiser and disliked the new Republic.

Exam practice

1 What does the graph above suggest about industrial output (shown in red) in the 1920s in Germany? *(4 marks)*

Exam tip For Exam practice question 1 above you can get up to two marks for quoting relevant bits from the source. The other two marks are for making inferences or deductions – that is, finding things that the source is suggesting without being openly stated.

Revision task

How had Germany changed by the end of the 1920s? Use a key word list to summarise the changes under the following headings:

	1921	1928
Economy		
International affairs		
Politics at home		

Exam practice

2 Explain Stresemann's successes in international relations 1924–29. *(6 marks)*

Exam tip For Exam practice question 1 above, you should aim to explain two or three factors (with some details) in order to reach the top level in the mark scheme.

8.3 How far did the Nazi Party develop its ideas and organisation up to 1929?

Hitler's early career

Before the 1920s, Hitler was not at all famous.

- He was born in Austria in 1889.
- As a young man, he lived in poverty in Vienna.
- He wanted to become a professional artist.
- In 1913, he went to live in Munich in Germany.
- When war broke out, he volunteered to join the German army.
- He was in the army throughout the war, was wounded twice, and won the Iron Cross – First Class, the highest award for a German soldier.
- In November 1918, he was in hospital recovering from being gassed, when he heard of Germany's surrender to the Allies.
- He was bitter, and blamed weak politicians, Jews and Communists for Germany's defeat.

The Party, 1919–23

In 1919, Hitler joined the German Workers' Party, which had been founded by Anton Drexler.

- He changed its name to the National Socialist German Workers' Party (Nazis) and took over as leader in 1921.
- He organised his own private army called the Sturm Abteilung (SA), or Stormtroopers, who were used to protect Nazi meetings and attack those of their opponents, especially the Communists.
- Hitler drew up a 25-point programme, which included the promise to reverse the terms of the Treaty of Versailles, destroy Communism and make Germany great. It also included an attack on the Jews, blaming them for Germany's defeat in the First World War.
- He attracted support from extreme nationalists and, by 1922, the Nazi Party had 3,000 members.

The Munich Putsch, November 1923

In November 1923, Hitler and the Nazis tried to seize control of Bavaria, an area with a large Nazi following. The plan was to capture Munich and from there march on Berlin. Hitler was convinced people would join him in overthrowing the failed Weimar Republic.

- On 8 November, Hitler forced members of the Bavarian Government to join him, at gunpoint. Its leader, Gustav Von Kahr, was reluctant to do so and alerted the army and the police.
- The Nazi plan soon began to go wrong. The next day, Bavarian police opened fire on Nazi Stormtroopers in Munich and sixteen Nazis were killed.
- Hitler and Ludendorff (the former First World War general who was now a Nazi supporter) were arrested and charged with high treason.

However, it was clear that Hitler's views had some support in Germany.
- Hitler received the minimum sentence. Many Nazi supporters also received light sentences.
- Hitler served his sentence in the comfortable Landsberg Fortress and spent his time writing his memoirs.
- The memoirs were later published as *Mein Kampf* (*My Struggle*). In this book, Hitler outlined his view of German history and his views on Germany's rightful place in the world.

The Munich Putsch became an important piece of Nazi propaganda when the Nazis gained power. Sources 3 and 4 show two differing accounts of Hitler's role in the events.

Which of these two sources on the right gives us the more reliable version of this event? To answer this, it is important to think about why they were written. Source 3 was written as a piece of Nazi propaganda and its purpose was to portray Hitler as a hero. The actions described are improbable, especially for someone who has sustained a serious injury. It is therefore unreliable as a piece of evidence.

Source 4, however, also has its problems. Rudolf Olden was a lawyer and a strong critic of Nazi policies in the 1930s. His evidence is so uncomplimentary about Hitler that we must be a little suspicious about this in the same way that we are about Source 3.

SOURCE 3
From the official biography of Hitler published by the Nazi Party in 1934.

The body of the man with whom Hitler was linked shot up in the air like a ball, tearing Hitler's arm with him, so that it sprang from the joint and fell back limp and dead … Hitler approached the man and stooped over him … a boy severely wounded. Blood was pouring from his mouth. Hitler picked him up and carried him on his shoulders.

SOURCE 4
Rudolf Olden, *Hitler the Pawn* (written in 1936). He was a German opponent of the Nazis and was living in exile.

At the first shot Hitler had flung himself to the ground. He sprained his arm, but this did not prevent him from running. He found his car and drove into the mountains.

Revision tasks

1 How did Hitler change the party in the period 1919–23?

2 Make a copy of the table below. Use key words to explain the causes, events and results of the Munich Putsch.

	The Munich Putsch
Causes	
Events	
Results	

Exam practice

1 Study Source 3 OR Source 4. How useful is this source for studying Hitler's role in the Munich Putsch? Use the source and your knowledge to explain your answer. (*10 marks*)

Exam tip For Exam practice question 1 above you should aim to write two paragraphs. One should be trying to assess how useful the source is likely to be, bearing in mind its likely purpose. The other should be about the content of the source – is it accurate? In both paragraphs you should provide some detailed explanation for a high mark.

The Nazi Party during the Stresemann years, 1924–29

This was a period of mixed fortunes for the Nazi Party. On the one hand, the Nazi Party did not do well.
- It won only twelve seats in the election of 1928.
- There were quarrels and disagreements within the party during Hitler's period in prison.

On the other hand, there was progress.
- Hitler had learned from the mistake of the Munich Putsch and was determined to achieve power through legal methods – by securing a majority of seats in the Reichstag.
- He reorganised the party to make it more efficient, setting up a headquarters in Munich and branches of the party all over Germany.

- Membership of the Nazi Party rose from 27,000 members in 1925 to over 100,000 in 1928.
- Some conservative people supported the Nazis when the party condemned the decadence of life in the cities.
- Many poor farmers supported the Nazi Party. They were not sharing in the increased prosperity of the Weimar Republic and the Nazis promised to help farming if they came to power.
- The SA was enlarged in size and the SS, a new group loyal to Hitler personally, was created.
- Nazi propaganda was controlled by Joseph Goebbels.

Revision task

Draw a line down the middle of a piece of paper. In one column, list the strengths of the Nazi Party by 1929. In the other column, list the weaknesses. In both columns you should consider the ideas of the Nazi Party, its organisation, and how much support it had by 1929.

Key content

You need to have a good working knowledge of the following areas. **Tick off each item** once you are confident in your knowledge.

- ❏ The end of the First World War and the effects of the Treaty of Versailles on Germany
- ❏ Political problems with the new constitution and political instability
- ❏ Attempted takeovers by the Spartacists and Freikorps; the Kapp Putsch
- ❏ Hyperinflation – causes and consequences; the invasion of the Ruhr
- ❏ The role of Stresemann as Chancellor and Foreign Minister
- ❏ Economic recovery with the new currency, the Dawes Plan and the Young Plan
- ❏ Germany's involvement diplomatically with the League of Nations
- ❏ The signing of the Locarno Pacts and the Kellogg–Briand Pact
- ❏ The extent of recovery in the late 1920s
- ❏ The early development of the Nazi Party
- ❏ The Munich Putsch and its consequences; *Mein Kampf*
- ❏ The extent of support for the Nazi Party in the later 1920s

Check your knowledge online with our Quick quizzes at www.hodderplus.co.uk/modernworldhistory.

After the First World War, people in Europe looked to the USA for leadership – both to help prevent future wars and for financial assistance. However, the USA failed to join the League of Nations, and only in the later 1920s provided any financial help to Germany.

Meanwhile, life within the USA flourished: the economy prospered, industry expanded rapidly with the onset of mass production, and people's lifestyles greatly improved. However, life for farmers and African Americans was not as easy, and by the end of the 1920s everyone's lives were affected by the financial collapse sparked by the Wall Street Crash.

Key issues

As with all examination topics, you will be expected to do more than simply learn the content and write it out again. You will need to show understanding of key issues from the period. These are:

- How and why did the USA achieve prosperity in the 1920s?
- How far was the USA a divided society in the 1920s?
- Why did the US stock exchange collapse in 1929?

9.1 How and why did the USA achieve prosperity in the 1920s?

Isolationism and its effects

The USA entered the First World War in 1917 with American soldiers fighting on the Western Front. President Woodrow Wilson played an important role at the peace talks. His Fourteen Points of 1918 (see page 18) were, in theory, the basis for the peace settlement. He was also responsible for setting up the League of Nations.

American attitudes

Most Americans were not keen on the League of Nations.
- They did not want their country involved in disputes taking place far away.
- They believed the USA would have to bear the cost of keeping the peace.

Reactions to the League

The American President was a Democrat but the rival party, the Republicans, controlled **Congress**. They were opposed to the League of Nations and refused to join. Wilson lost the presidential election of 1920 to the Republican Warren Harding. Harding fought the election with the slogan 'America First'. He talked of the need to return to 'normalcy', a word he had invented to convey the idea of getting life back to normal, as it was before the war. In addition, the League was intended to uphold the terms of the Treaty of Versailles. Since the USA did not

> **Key term**
>
> **Congress:** the American representative assemblies (the equivalent of Parliament in Britain). There are two houses, the Senate and the House of Representatives.

join the League, it meant that in practice Americans had opted out of taking any responsibility for the terms of the treaty.

Therefore, the USA started the 1920s politically isolated from Europe, with no treaty commitments. This policy was also taken in foreign trade and immigration.

Throughout the 1920s, Republican presidents were in power, and they implemented Republican policies. President Harding's key policies were isolation, tariffs and low taxes to help businesses to grow, and to give workers money to spend. When Harding died suddenly in 1923, Vice-President Coolidge succeeded him and followed the same policies.

> ## Cross reference
> *For more detail on the setting up of the League of Nations, see Chapter 2, pages 22–3.*

Revision task

In two columns, list the arguments for and against the USA joining the League of Nations if you were:
- a Democrat supporting President Wilson
- a Republican supporting Warren Harding.

Tariff policy: the Fordney–McCumber tariff, 1922

The American Government made sure that foreign goods did not compete with home-produced goods. In 1922, Congress passed the Fordney–McCumber tariff.
- This put a tariff (tax) on foreign goods and made them more expensive than the same American products.
- The policy was intended to protect American industry and worked well in the 1920s. It helped to create 'boom' conditions.
- The tariff was not so effective in the long term as it encouraged foreign governments to retaliate and put tariffs on American goods.

Mass production

1. The background: the USA before 1920

The USA's industry and farming had grown steadily since the 1860s.
- The country had huge resources (coal, iron, timber, oil).
- It had a growing population, many of them immigrants willing to work hard.
- Railways, mining and manufacturing were all strong.

In the early years of the First World War, American businesses profited from the war in Europe.
- American industries supplied arms and equipment.
- American firms were able to take over much of the export business of the European powers while they were caught up in the fighting.

The First World War made the USA wealthy and confident. Americans felt they were doing well. It also made them isolationist. They did not want to be dragged into Europe's wars.

2. Mass production techniques

In the 1920s, the profits of many American companies rose enormously. More goods were produced more quickly and cheaply because of new mass-production techniques.

The assembly line had been pioneered by Henry Ford before the First World War. He founded the Ford Motor Company in 1903, and by 1914 was beginning to use a moving assembly line. Workers could specialise in one part of the process of car manufacture. This meant that:
- a car could be produced in nearly one-tenth of the time previously taken
- the price of cars came down
- wages for production-line workers went up.

The motor industry was the single most important industry in the USA. More and more people could afford to buy cars, and by 1930 there were 30 million in the USA. This huge level of demand stimulated other industries (for example, metal, rubber and electrical industries). Indeed, the jobs of 4 million people depended on the motor industry, directly or indirectly.

Because of mass production methods, industrial production almost doubled during the 1920s without any increase in the size of the workforce. The textiles industry was changing with the introduction of synthetic materials such as rayon. The demand for electric power escalated, and by the end of the 1920s electricity supply was organised in large regional grids for much of the USA.

The construction industry boomed, with the rapid growth in the number and size of skyscrapers in cities such as New York. The Empire State Building was regarded as one of the wonders of the modern world.

3. Consumer industries and advertising

The biggest boom came in the industries making consumer goods – goods for ordinary families to buy. Sales of household goods, such as vacuum cleaners and washing machines, boosted the electrical industry.

There was a huge increase in advertising with the development of mail-order catalogues, as well as billboards, newspapers and the growing medium of radio. Advertising, credit and hire purchase (see below) made it easy to spend. Wages for many Americans rose, and there was a feeling of confidence, as Source 1 shows.

Comment

Henry Ford was a pacifist (he did not believe in war), but he made a lot of money producing armaments for the American armed forces in the First World War. He was also very anti-Jewish, and claimed that Jewish American bankers had too much influence. However, he also built a hospital, funded an orphanage and gave lots of money to help education.

Exam Practice

1 How useful is **Source 1** for studying the living standards of Americans in the late 1920s? Use the source and your knowledge to explain your answer. *(10 marks)*

SOURCE 1

President Hoover in a speech in 1928.

We in America are nearer to the final victory over poverty than ever before in the history of any land.

Exam tip

In thinking about Exam practice question 1 on the left, you need to consider:
- whether you agree or not with the content of the source
- how the fact that it is from a speech by the US President may affect its accuracy.

Finance in the 1920s: hire purchase, shares and the stock market boom

Sales benefited enormously in the 1920s from the use of hire purchase – people paying a deposit and then paying off the rest in instalments. This was helped by the relatively low rates of interest charged by banks. The explosion in consumer demand helped factories expand, which in turn meant more jobs were available. The economy was booming!

Many people bought shares in companies as investments. With increasing demand, the prices of shares went up and up. People believed that their value would continue to rise, and were therefore willing to borrow money from banks in order to buy shares, often using their house as a guarantee. Banks themselves were willing to lend more than they actually had, confident that with rising share prices values would go up sufficiently before investors wanted to withdraw their savings. (This is called buying shares 'on the margin'.)

The Republican governments of the 1920s believed in two main policies:
- laissez-faire – interfering in business as little as possible
- **rugged individualism** – believing that individuals were responsible for their own lives.

During the 1920s, the stock market boomed. On average, share prices went up 300 per cent.

Key term

Rugged individualism: the notion that people should overcome problems and succeed by their own efforts and hard work, not by receiving help from the Government.

Developments in the entertainment industries

During the 1920s, films became a national obsession. Millions of Americans went to the cinema each week to watch new stars such as Buster Keaton and Charlie Chaplin. Hollywood became the centre of a multi-million dollar industry. At the same time, jazz music became a craze and the USA became the centre of the world entertainment industry.

Both radio and gramophone records helped jazz music to spread more widely. Radio stations also helped to increase the popularity of sports. Rapidly increasing car ownership helped people to travel to sports fixtures, either as players or spectators. New dances became popular, such as the Charleston, the tango and the black bottom. These were seen as being in conflict with more traditional and restrained dances.

9.2 How far was the USA a divided society in the 1920s?

Rich versus poor

There was a huge contrast in the USA in the 1920s between rich and poor. In early 1929, five per cent of the population enjoyed about one-third of the nation's wealth. However, over half of American families lived below what was accepted as the poverty line.

- Farmers had a hard time in the 1920s. They produced more food than was needed and, as a result, prices fell. This led to reduced incomes, with many farmers unable to keep up their mortgage payments. Some farmers were evicted and others were forced to sell their land.
- African Americans had a similar experience. Almost 1 million lost their jobs in the 1920s. Many moved to the north where they found lower-paid jobs.
- Not all industries benefited from the boom. For example, the coal industry declined due to competition from new forms of power such as electricity and gas. There were wage cuts and job losses in the coal and cotton industries.
- Many children worked long hours in textile factories and in agriculture for very low wages.

Race: immigration controls

In the decades before the First World War, millions of Europeans and some Asians emigrated to the USA. The country was seen as a 'melting pot' of nationalities and races. A city such as New York was truly international in appearance and in speech. Many of those from Europe were from the south and east, speaking languages far removed from English and German; they were mostly Catholic; and often had little education. Therefore, there were growing fears about the consequences of an 'open' policy for immigrants, even before the 1920s.

- Immigrants provided cheap labour and therefore created competition for jobs.
- Immigrants might bring new political ideas, such as Communism from Russia, which would threaten American democracy.
- There was also racial prejudice against those who were not white-skinned and did not originate from northern Europe.
- Recent waves of immigrants were tending to concentrate in **ghettos** within cities, where crime and violence were high.

> **Revision task**
>
> Imagine you are growing up in a wealthy family in the USA in the 1920s. First, describe your life as a wealthy teenager. Next, describe what life was like for your parents when they grew up a generation earlier.

> **Key term**
>
> **Ghetto:** a very poor area of a city lived in by a minority group that experiences discrimination or segregation.

In the 1920s, Congress therefore passed various laws to limit the number of immigrants.

1917 Immigration Law	Required all foreigners to take a literacy test to prove they could read a short passage of English. This effectively prevented people from poorer countries entering the USA.
1921 Immigration Quota Act	This limited the maximum number of immigrants allowed into the USA to 357,000 per year. It also limited the number of each ethnic group emigrating to the USA to three per cent of the number already in the USA in 1910. This worked in favour of immigrants from northern and western Europe as they already had a great number of American citizens.
1924 National Origins Act	This further reduced the quota to two per cent of the population in 1890.
1929 Immigration Act	The number of immigrants entering the USA each year was reduced to 150,000.

Revision task

Study **Source 2** below. Do the figures in the chart confirm what is said about the effects of the Acts of 1921 and 1924 relating to immigration in the USA? Explain your answer.

SOURCE 2

	Effects	
	1921	1924
Number of immigrants restricted to:	3% of 1910 population	2% of 1890 population
UK/Ireland	77,342	62,574
Germany/Austria	75,510	52,012
Eastern Europe	63,191	10,902
Italy	42,957	3,845

Quota levels of immigrants to the USA.

Exam practice

1 Explain how the USA controlled immigration in the 1920s. *(6 marks)*

Exam tip For Exam practice question 1 on the left, you should aim to explain two or three factors (with some details) in order to reach the top level in the mark scheme.

The Ku Klux Klan

Although slavery had been abolished during the American Civil War (1861–65), African Americans did not have equal rights. **Segregation** was legal in the southern states. In 1896, the US Supreme Court had given legal approval for what became known as the **Jim Crow** Laws – that is, treating African Americans as inferior, to be exploited by whites Americans.

The Ku Klux Klan (KKK) had originally been formed in 1866. Its intention was to terrorise African Americans who had just gained their freedom in the American Civil War.

- In 1915, the organisation was re-formed, and attacked Catholics and Jews as well as African Americans. In the early 1920s it was hugely popular, with 5 million members.

- Many white Americans were afraid of what they saw as the negative consequences of the racial and cultural mix of the USA. Many recent immigrants were from southern and eastern Europe and mostly Catholic rather than Protestant in religion. Many Jews had fled Europe before and during the First World War. This added to the existing fears about African American people diluting what was seen as 'pure' American culture. KKK supporters believed that the USA's greatness was founded on the achievements of WASPS (White Anglo-Saxon Protestants). Other cultures were seen as inferior.

- Klansmen met in secret at night, but sometimes paraded openly during the day, wearing white hoods and white sheets. They intended to terrorise African Americans and other hated groups, such as Jews and Catholics, into accepting inferior status under the control of the WASPs. The 'Imperial Wizard' led the Klan, with a 'Grand Dragon' in charge in each state.

- African American people feared the KKK. They suffered acts of violence, such as being beaten, raped or even lynched. The courts were on the side of white Americans as many police and judges were members of the KKK.

The influence of the KKK decreased in the later 1920s. A well-publicised court case led to one of its leaders being convicted of the kidnap, rape and murder of a woman on a train. Even so, there was still much racism in the USA.

Key terms

Segregation: keeping a group separate from the rest of society, usually on the basis of race or religion. Segregation was seen in separate schools, transport and housing.

Jim Crow: the name Jim Crow was made popular by a white American comedian who made fun of African Americans. Originally, Jim Crow was a character in an old song. This name became linked to the southern laws ensuring that African American people remained inferior.

Exam practice

2 How useful is **Source 3** for studying the activities of the KKK in the 1920s? Use the source and your knowledge to explain your answer. *(10 marks)*

SOURCE 3

R. A. Patton, writing about the actions of the Ku Klux Klan in Alabama, in *Current History*, 1929.

A lad whipped with branches until his back was ribboned flesh ... a white girl, divorcee, beaten into unconsciousness in her home; a naturalised foreigner flogged until his back was pulp because he married an American woman; a negro lashed until he sold his land to a white man for a fraction of its value.

Exam tip For Exam practice question 2 on the left you should aim to write two paragraphs. One should be trying to assess how useful the source is likely to be, bearing in mind its likely purpose. The other should be about the content of the source – is it accurate? In both paragraphs you should provide some detailed explanation for a high mark.

Prohibition

Prohibition: how it was introduced

Some groups were strongly in favour of prohibiting the sale of alcoholic drinks. There was a strong temperance (anti-alcohol) movement in the USA. Some states within the USA had voted for prohibition before the First World War. During the war, there were additional arguments in its support.

- Drinking alcohol became associated with absenteeism from work.
- The main beers drunk in the USA were German, and it was said to be unpatriotic to be drinking German beer during the war.

By the end of the war, three-quarters of the states in America had prohibited the manufacture and sale of alcoholic drinks. With this wide support across the USA, temperance groups pressured the Government to introduce prohibition nationwide. This involved passing an amendment to the Constitution – the Eighteenth Amendment.

Many Americans celebrated the banning of 'the demon drink', and expected that it would help to reduce social abuses such as family neglect. Those against prohibition accepted that the law had been passed, but did not necessarily intend to obey it.

Prohibition: problems of enforcement

Prohibition was not a success because it was impossible to enforce.

- The alcohol trade was driven underground.
- **Bootleggers** made large amounts of money smuggling alcohol into the USA.
- There was much illegal brewing of alcohol – **moonshine** – within the USA.
- Speakeasies (illegal bars) opened up and sold beer and other drinks.
- The Government appointed prohibition agents, but they were far too few in number.
- Two of the agents, Izzy Einstein and Moe Smith, gained a reputation for wearing elaborate disguises. They raided 3,000 speakeasies in the first half of the 1920s.

Prohibition and crime

Gangs of criminals began to run bootlegging schemes and other forms of crime (gambling, drugs, prostitution) like a business. The gangs would sometimes fight each other for control of the trade. They controlled the speakeasies by running protection rackets, and the police often dared not intervene.

The most notorious gang leader was Al Capone. He virtually controlled the city of Chicago by bribing the mayor and other politicians. He employed nearly 1,000 men, many of them with guns. Violence was used when it was considered necessary, and over 200 murders have been linked to gang activities. The most famous massacre was in 1929 when some of Al Capone's gang gunned down six members of the rival Bugs Moran gang (the St Valentine's Day massacre).

The end of prohibition

After the Wall Street Crash and with high unemployment and much misery, it was easier to argue for the end of prohibition – the end of the 'noble experiment'. One effect of ending prohibition would be the creation of legal jobs. In the 1932 presidential election campaign, F. D. Roosevelt promised to **repeal** the law. This involved Congress passing another amendment to the Constitution, the Twenty-First, and it came into effect in 1933.

Comment

Al Capone used his gangs and financial influence to control the illegal liquor trade and to influence politics, yet he also gave generously to charities. He was never brought to trial for his violence and murders. However, during the 1930s he spent eight years in prison for not paying taxes.

Key terms

Bootleggers: people who carried liquor into the USA from Canada or Mexico. The name comes from the fact that they sometimes hid the bottles inside their knee-length boots.

Moonshine: illegal liquor, often made or distributed under cover of darkness.

Repeal: to cancel an original law by an Act passed by Congress.

Young people

Many young people gained more freedom in the 1920s. This was partly as a result of more transport being available and having more money to spend. However, it also reflected a change in attitudes among the younger generation.

The group that attracted particular attention was the flappers. These young ladies wore short skirts, had short hair, put on make-up, and did what were considered outrageous things, such as smoking in public and dancing the tango and the Charleston. The older generations, especially those living in rural areas of the USA, were shocked by these developments.

SOURCE 4

"WHAT WILL YOU TAKE, BOYS?"

A poster issued by the Women's Christian Temperance Union.

SOURCE 5

From an American magazine, 1925.

Statistics in the Detroit police court of 1924 show 7,391 arrests for violations of the prohibition law; but only 450 convictions. Ten years ago a dishonest policeman was a rarity. Now the honest ones are pointed out as rarities. Their relationship with the bootleggers is perfectly friendly. They have to arrest two out of five once in a while, but they choose the ones who are least willing to pay bribes.

9.3 Why did the US stock exchange collapse in 1929?

The problems of the 1920s

Historians can identify long- and short-term causes of the collapse in 1929. The longer-term causes stem from the weaknesses and underlying problems of the American economy during the 1920s.

Long-term causes

- Over-production in agriculture drove prices down.
- Over-production in consumer goods did the same, and once families had bought these goods (for example, refrigerators), they did not need more.
- Lack of credit control meant that investors were encouraged to speculate and rely on share prices continuing to rise. There was a lack of regulation to control business activities.

- The effects of the tariff policy, where America restricted imports by high tariffs, encouraged other countries to retaliate – this made it difficult for the USA to export surplus goods.
- The unequal distribution of wealth, with over half the population having very limited ability to make purchases or invest, reduced the size of the American market.

Short-term causes

Short-term causes related to shares. Many ordinary Americans bought shares in companies. Normally this is good for business. However, in the USA in the 1920s the rush to buy shares caused problems.

- Many people bought and sold shares to make quick profits instead of keeping their money invested in the same businesses for some time. They were speculators, not investors.
- Companies were forced by shareholders to pay out profits to shareholders rather than reinvesting the profits.
- Americans borrowed money on credit to buy their shares.

These kinds of share dealing depended on confidence that share prices would continue to rise. Once people started worrying about the long-term weaknesses in the American economy, disaster struck. In September 1929, the prices of shares began to edge down – slowly to start with – but people soon began to realise that the shares they owned were worth less than the loans they had used to buy them in the first place. All of a sudden, everyone tried to get rid of their shares, selling them for less and less. The worst day was 'Black Tuesday', 29 October 1929. As a result, share prices collapsed.

Exam practice

1 What does **Source 6** suggest about the effects of the Wall Street Crash of October 1929? *(4 marks)*

SOURCE 6

Company	Share value in cents		
	3 Sept 1928	**3 Sept 1929**	**13 Nov 1929**
New York Central	256	256	160
Union Carbide and Carbon	413	137	59
Electric Bond and Share	203	186	50

Share prices, 1928–29 (from the *Wall Street Journal*).

Exam tip For Exam practice question 1 on the left you can get up to two marks for quoting relevant bits from the source. The other two marks are for making inferences or deductions – that is, finding things that the source is suggesting without being openly stated.

The immediate consequences of the crash

The effects of the crash were disastrous.

- Many individuals were bankrupt – they could not pay back the loans they used to buy their (now worthless) shares.
- Some homeowners lost their homes as they could not pay their mortgages.
- Even some of those who had savings lost their money when banks collapsed.
- Many farmers suffered a similar fate as banks tried to get back their loans.

The confidence of individuals was shattered. Many faced unemployment, and those in work faced reduced hours and wages. They tightened their belts and stopped spending.
   Big institutions also suffered.

- About 11,000 banks stopped trading between 1929 and 1933.
- At the same time, demand for goods of all types fell.
- As a result, production fell and so did wages and jobs.

Unemployment rose dramatically, as shown in the diagram below.

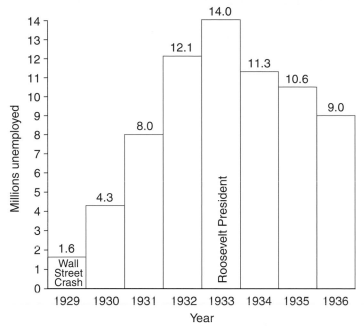

Unemployment, 1929–36.

Most Americans blamed Hoover for the crash, even though this was unfair as he had only just become President and had merely continued the policies of previous Republican governments under Presidents Harding and Coolidge. However, Hoover did anger many people by his insistence at first that the situation was not too serious – 'prosperity is just around the corner'.

Revision tasks

1 List the main causes of the collapse of the stock exchange in 1929.
2 In your view, what were the most important causes, and why?

Key content

You need to have a good working knowledge of the following areas.
Tick off each item once you are confident in your knowledge.

- ❏ The USA's rejection of the Treaty of Versailles and refusal to join the League of Nations
- ❏ The consequence of isolationism, including the Fordney–McCumber tariff policy
- ❏ Mass production; developments in consumer industries and advertising
- ❏ The stock market boom, including government policies towards share purchase
- ❏ The developments in entertainment industries such as cinema and jazz
- ❏ The contrast between rich and poor, e.g. farmers
- ❏ Immigration controls through laws
- ❏ The activities and effect of the Ku Klux Klan
- ❏ The reasons for and against Prohibition; the consequences for society
- ❏ Fashion and flappers in the 1920s
- ❏ The conditions leading to the Stock Market collapse in 1929
- ❏ The events and immediate consequences of the Wall Street Crash

Check your knowledge online with our Quick quizzes at www.hodderplus.co.uk/modernworldhistory.

After the death of Lenin in 1924, there was a power struggle in the USSR in the later 1920s. By 1929, Stalin was in total command, and in the 1930s he tightened his grip through censorship, propaganda and purges of possible opponents. Meanwhile, he aimed to make the USSR a great economic power through the modernisation of agriculture and the utilisation of the country's natural resources to achieve rapid growth in heavy industries such as coal, metal and electricity. By 1941, when Germany invaded the USSR, sufficient progress had been made for the USSR to resist its invaders.

Key issues

As with all examination topics, you will be expected to do more than simply learn the content and write it out again. You will need to show understanding of key issues from the period. These are:

- To what extent had Stalin become a personal dictator in Communist Russia by the end of the 1920s?
- How did Stalin reinforce his dictatorship in the 1930s?
- To what extent did Stalin make the USSR a great economic power?

10.1 To what extent had Stalin become a personal dictator in Communist Russia by the end of the 1920s?

The death and funeral of Lenin

Although he was only in his early fifties, Lenin had suffered a series of strokes in 1922 and 1923. He became speechless, and died in January 1924. The loss of Lenin at so early a stage in the development of the USSR was a big shock to those working under him. The Civil War had only just ended; NEP was in its infancy; and the USSR, uniting all the different nations within the Russian Empire, had only just been created.

Lenin had been seen as the hero of the establishment of Communism. Soon after his death, the city of Petrograd was renamed Leningrad in his honour.

The background of Stalin and Trotsky

Stalin and Trotsky were the main contenders to replace Lenin as leader. Stalin had not played an important part in the Communist revolution of 1917, but he had become important in Lenin's Government.

- Stalin's origins were humble. He was the son of a shoemaker in Georgia.
- He had become a Bolshevik and had taken part in various illegal activities, such as robbing a bank. He had a reputation for being ruthless.

Cross reference

For details of what was happening in the years before the death of Lenin, see Chapter 7, pages 72–76. This will be especially useful if you are not studying Lenin as part of your depth studies.

- In 1917, Stalin had been a loyal supporter of Lenin on the Bolshevik Central Committee.
- After the Communist revolution of 1917, Stalin had worked his way up to the position of General Secretary of the Party, and established a reputation as being a good organiser.
- He hated intellectuals – he preferred simple, practical ideas.

Trotsky was very different in background and experience.
- He was born to Jewish farmers in the Ukraine.
- He was very clever as a boy, and developed revolutionary ideas, as shown in his many writings.
- In the years before 1917 he was living abroad in exile, publishing books and newspapers.
- After the Tsar abdicated in March 1917, Trotsky returned to Russia and joined the Bolshevik Party. In September 1917, he became the Chairman of the Petrograd Soviet (workers' council).
- He took charge of the actual planning that led to Communist success, including taking the Winter Palace in October/November 1917.
- Under Lenin, Trotsky was Commissar for War, and created the Red Army of 3 million men that defeated the Whites in the Civil War.

The other, less significant, contenders to take over as leader were Bukharin, Zinoviev and Kamenev.

Lenin's *Testament*

In 1922, after his first stroke, Lenin became concerned about what would happen to the leadership of the party after his death. So he dictated his thoughts in a document that has become known as his *Testament*. In January 1923, he added a postscript that was critical of Stalin.

After Lenin's death, Stalin persuaded the other leading Bolsheviks that publishing the document would not be in the interests of party unity. They agreed for a variety of reasons – for example, Kamenev and Zinoviev, who had been loyal Bolsheviks for many years, resented Lenin's praise of Trotsky. Lenin's wife, Krupskaya, was overruled in her desire to see the document published.

Stalin's claims to power

- Stalin had been a loyal Bolshevik for many years under Lenin. He made sure that he was seen as Lenin's right-hand man. This even included doctoring photographs of Lenin to show Stalin at his right-hand side.
- He organised Lenin's funeral.
- He was an excellent organiser and controlled the party machine as General Secretary.
- He wanted to build up Communism in the USSR first, before thinking of expanding its influence beyond.

Trotsky's claims to power

- He had carried out the Bolshevik takeover of October/November 1917.
- He had created and led the Red Army to victory over the Whites in the Civil War.
- He was an enthusiastic writer and speaker, and wanted Communism to spread to all developed countries as quickly as possible, following the teaching of Karl Marx. His belief in world revolution clashed with Stalin's policy of 'socialism in one country'.

Communist rule in the later 1920s

Following Lenin's death there was no automatic leader. Leadership was, in theory, shared amongst the nine members of the **Politburo**. The Union of Soviet Socialist Republics (USSR) had been created shortly before Lenin's death, and this incorporated all the non-Russian areas that had been part of the Russian Empire. Many of these areas resented this as they had looked forward to regaining or gaining their independence after the collapse of the Tsar's Russian Empire.

Censorship had already been imposed under Lenin. The Bolsheviks had many enemies, thus books, newspapers and films were limited. Propaganda techniques were developing. Statues and paintings of Lenin appeared all over the country.

The power struggle between Stalin and Trotsky

- Stalin used Lenin's funeral to advance his own position. He took on the role of chief mourner. Trotsky was not present. He had been recuperating from illness in the warm south of the USSR, and Stalin deliberately told him the wrong date for the funeral so he could not attend.
- Lenin's *Testament*, which criticised Stalin, was not made public.
- Stalin published a book three months after Lenin's death called *The Foundations of Leninism*. In this, he praised and publicised Lenin's ideas.
- Stalin used his position as General Secretary to appoint his own supporters as junior officials. These Stalin-supporters elected the Politburo.
- Stalin also became editor of the party newspaper, *Pravda*.
- Trotsky suffered for being a Jew (there was a lot of anti-Semitism at the time).
- Stalin's wish to build up Communism in the USSR was contrasted with Trotsky's belief in moving quickly towards world revolution. Stalin's policy appealed to war-weary Russians. Most leading Communists agreed with Stalin.
- In 1925, Trotsky was dismissed from his post as Commissar for War.
- Trotsky wanted to revolutionise agriculture (as Stalin set out to do a few years later), but Stalin gained support for his policy of continuing Lenin's NEP.
- In 1926, Trotsky, Kamenev and Zinoviev were dismissed from the Politburo – the leading Bolshevik committee.
- In 1927, Zinoviev and Trotsky were expelled from the Communist Party.
- By 1928, Stalin and his supporters controlled the Politburo.
- In 1929, Trotsky was expelled from the USSR. Stalin was in control.

Revision task

Sources 1 and **2** give some views on Stalin. They were written before Stalin had achieved total control. In what ways do these sources predict the rise of Stalin?

SOURCE 1

John Reed, an American Communist who lived in Russia, writing in his book *Ten Days that Shook the World*.

He's [Stalin] not the intellectual like the other people you will meet. He's not even particularly well informed but he knows what he wants. He's got willpower and he's going to be on top of the pile some day.

SOURCE 2

Trotsky on Stalin.

I said to Smirnov: 'Stalin will become the dictator of the USSR.' 'Stalin?' he asked me with amazement. 'But he is a mediocrity, a colourless nonentity.' 'Mediocrity, yes, nonentity, no … He is needed by all of them – the tired radicals, the bureaucrats, the NEP men, the kulaks [wealthier peasant farmers], the upstarts …

Key term

Politburo: the group of Bolsheviks (Communists) in charge of policy-making.

Comment

'Pravda' means 'truth'. You can guess that the version of events described in this newspaper only contained one side of the truth!

Exam practice

1 'Stalin was bound to become dictator after the death of Lenin. There was no other choice.' How far do you agree with this interpretation? Explain your answer.

(12 marks)

Exam tip Question 1 above is a typical style of essay question used in the exams. First, prepare an answer in brief note form, jotting down reasons to agree and reasons to disagree. Then think how you can develop your ideas into longer arguments. Finally, consider what conclusion you might reach about the interpretation.

10.2 How did Stalin reinforce his dictatorship in the 1930s?

The control of the Communist Party

Stalin controlled, through the Politburo, all the departments of government. His secret police intruded everywhere, and aimed to stop all criticism of Stalin and his policies. It changed its name several times, but the one that is most associated with the rule of Stalin is the NKVD (People's Commissariat of Internal Affairs).

The constitution of 1936

The new **constitution** *appeared* to give rights and some freedom to the people of the USSR. However, the NKVD was allowed to ignore the guarantees written down in the constitution.

Although the **Supreme Soviet** was elected by everyone aged eighteen and over in a secret ballot, the only candidates were Communist Party members.

The purges

From 1934 to 1938, millions of people were arrested, imprisoned, murdered or simply disappeared. This is collectively known as 'the purges', with Stalin getting rid of anyone opposing him, suspected of opposing him, or possibly going to oppose him in the future.

1. The reasons for the purges

Stalin could have relied on the NKVD to deal with criticism and suspected opposition, but he went much further than that with the purges. The exact reasons have been a matter of debate. Here are some suggestions:

- Stalin suffered from paranoia.
- He liked cruelty.
- Stalin was alarmed by some of the 'old Bolsheviks' who were cleverer than he was and could weaken his position.
- Stalin was afraid of Kirov (see below).
- The purges could be used as a means of explaining failures and shortcomings if people were found guilty of plotting against the Communist state.
- They helped to unify the nation by appealing to nationalist values. This was particularly important in the later 1930s as Hitler threatened eastern Europe.

2. The extent of the purges

In December 1934, Sergei Kirov, a member of the Politburo and a close friend of Stalin, was murdered. It is now believed by most people that Kirov was killed on the orders of Stalin himself.

However, at the time it provided an excuse to announce the existence of a conspiracy, and leading Communists, such as Kamenev and Zinoviev, were arrested on false charges. Anyone feared by Stalin – for whatever reason – could be arrested, imprisoned, sent to a labour camp (*gulag*) or executed.

3. Show trials

A series of 'show trials', which started in 1936, featured ridiculous accusations against leading Communists. The biggest trial was that of Zinoviev, Kamenev and fourteen others. Film of the trial was sent abroad. People were shocked to see the state prosecutor, Andrei Vyshinsky, questioning these famous people – and gaining confessions of guilt by intimidation.

Within the USSR, the trials were reported on the radio and in local newspapers. Ordinary workers were encouraged to demonstrate in favour of harsh punishments for the guilty. Most of the accused were shot.

> ### Key terms
>
> **Constitution:** an agreed method of governing a country, with the details usually written down and agreed on by those being governed.
>
> **Supreme Soviet:** an elected body of representatives (the equivalent of the British Parliament), but which had no real power. It only met for two weeks a year. It was the Communist Party under Stalin that made the important decisions.

> **Exam tip** It is important to see that Stalin's dictatorship increased from the 1920s into the 1930s, so that by the mid-1930s it was very difficult for any citizen to resist.

Further show trials in 1937 and 1938 repeated the procedure. However, in the same period, nearly 1 million other officials of lesser ranks were accused of serious crimes. They were either imprisoned, sent to labour camps or shot. Even the NKVD was affected. Its leader, Yagoda, was found guilty and shot.

4. The Great Terror

Millions of people across the USSR were arrested and either sent to labour camps or shot. They came from all classes of society – both the educated and the workers. The NKVD was feared everywhere. Sometimes those in the NKVD were simply given targets for the number of people to be arrested.

Conditions in the labour camps were appalling. Many people died of cold, malnutrition or disease. Working conditions were also brutal with a lack of proper machinery for doing heavy jobs.

The extent of this terror is disputed, but many historians agree that more than 10 million people died as a direct or indirect consequence of the Great Terror.

5. The purging of the armed forces

In 1937, around 25,000 army officers (including the Commander of the Red Army, Marshal Tukhachevsky) were purged. All six Admirals of the Soviet Navy and most of the Air Force commanders were shot. Other lower ranks were also affected.

SOURCE 3

The fate of the Bolshevik leaders of 1917. From a newspaper published by supporters of Trotsky in 1938.

> **Comment**
>
> *Note that there are obvious parallels (and differences) between Stalin's methods of dictatorship and those developed by Hitler in the same years.*

> **Exam practice**
>
> **1** Study **Source 3**. Explain why leading Bolsheviks were purged in the 1930s.
>
> *(8 marks)*
>
> **2** Why do you think Stalin was able to preside over the horrors of the purges and Great Terror and still be seen as a great leader by many people within the USSR and abroad?
>
> *(8 marks)*

> **Exam tip** For Exam practice questions 1 and 2 above, you should aim to explain two or three causes (with some details) in order to reach the top level in the mark scheme.

6. The consequences of the purges

- The number of Communist Party members fell from 3.5 million in 1934 to 2 million in 1935.
- Those killed were not the only ones affected. People's families were threatened and they lived in constant fear.
- Stalin was secure in his dictatorship. The NKVD ruled the population with terror.

- Stalin had weakened the USSR intellectually. Many of those purged had been educated or skilled in industry. Industrial progress slowed down.
- Stalin weakened the ability of the USSR to defend itself at a crucial time in the late 1930s. The army was still recovering from the purges when German armies attacked the USSR in June 1941.

The cult of personality

Stalin was portrayed as a hero with tremendous achievements. Films were made in celebration of his rule. Poetry and music aimed to enhance his glory. Posters and statues showed Stalin in victorious poses, often mixing with happy workers. Indeed, many posters featured the alleged successes of agriculture and industry. Stalin was hailed as 'The Leader of Genius of the Toilers of the Whole World'. What was being created was a personality cult.

Censorship was tightened. Anything published that was in the least way critical of Stalin resulted in severe punishment. In 1932, the Union of Soviet Writers was set up. Its job was to ensure that novels featured Soviet heroes and happy endings. The most famous writer to suffer was Alexander Solzhenitsyn, who spent many years in labour camps.

Musicians were also controlled. Dmitri Shostakovich was the most famous of these, and he sometimes felt compelled to write pieces in heroic mood that celebrated the achievements of Communism. Art and sculpture also had to show heroes and a spirit of optimism.

To enforce Stalin's dictatorship, the NKVD had spies everywhere. Anyone could be arrested and punished with little or no real evidence against them. Interrogation could be vicious and would lead to harsh sentences in a labour camp. In these camps, the working conditions were terrible with only basic food and shelter and the expectation of hard physical labour.

Education was controlled by the NKVD, as Source 4 shows.

SOURCE 4

Nadezhda Mandelstam, a Russian writer.

She showed us her school textbooks where the portraits of party leaders had thick pieces of paper pasted over them as one by one they fell into disgrace – this the children had to do on instructions from their teacher … With every new arrest, people went through their books and burned the works of disgraced leaders in their stoves.

SOURCE 5

Comrade Stalin and the Peoples of the USSR. Painted in 1937 by Vasilii Vakovlev and Petr Shukhmin. It shows Stalin applauding his people.

Revision task

Using **Sources 4** and **5** and your own knowledge, list the methods by which a cult of personality was created in the USSR in the 1930s, and write a sentence about each.

10.3 To what extent did Stalin make the USSR a great economic power?

The economic situation in the USSR in the late 1920s

In the late 1920s, the USSR was still very backward economically.

- Industrial output had barely recovered to the levels of 1913 before the First World War.
- Lenin had started NEP with some initial success, but it was unlikely to achieve the rapid transformation that Stalin said was needed.

Stalin's aim was to force the USSR to make fifty years' progress in ten years. This was essential to show off Communism, but also to enable the USSR to prepare to defend itself from the threatened invasion by capitalist countries. The changes were to be forced through by modernising agriculture and imposing ambitious targets for industry in Five-Year Plans.

Farming: the need for collectivisation

Stalin had made clear his ambitions to transform the USSR. The Five-Year Plans could work only if Soviet agriculture could raise its production massively. There were two main reasons for doing this.

- To feed the growing population of industrial workers.
- To export any surpluses to raise cash for investment in industry.

How collectivisation worked

Most farms were smallholdings tended by peasant families. These holdings could never be efficient enough for Stalin's plans so he introduced the policy of collectivisation.

- Peasants effectively had to give up their land and join other families on very large farms.
- These new farms were supplied by the state with seed, tools, tractors and other machinery.
- Most of the produce went to the Government.

The real opponents of collectivisation were the kulaks. Kulaks were peasants who had become prosperous under the NEP, and they made up a large and important part of the population of the countryside. Most refused to co-operate with the new policy because they did not want to give up their land.

The effects of collectivisation

The effects of collectivisation were very mixed, but this policy certainly had less claim to success than the Five-Year Plans. This is what happened.

- By 1941, almost all land in the USSR was collectivised.
- A huge propaganda campaign was launched to convince peasants to modernise.
- Many peasants and kulaks killed their animals rather than hand them over to the Government. The number of pigs and cattle halved in the years 1928–33. Grain production fell from 73 million tonnes to 69 million tonnes in the same years.
- Kulaks were murdered or put in labour camps.
- Much of the countryside was devastated by struggles between Stalin's agents and the kulaks.
- Although collectivisation was achieved, food production fell dramatically. In the Ukraine, there was famine in the early 1930s and at the same time food was being exported.

The long-term result of this struggle was that the peasants were battered into submission and never again seriously threatened the Communist regime.

Industrialisation

The Five-Year Plans

Stalin seemed to have several clear reasons for industrialising the USSR. These were:

- security
- to create a showpiece of success for the outside world
- to carry out his idea of 'socialism in one country'.

In order to achieve his aims, he came up with two Five-Year Plans for the development of the USSR. They presented incredibly ambitious targets for industrial production that had to be achieved in five years.

Although few targets were met (see diagram, above), the industries that failed to meet their targets still made huge advances.

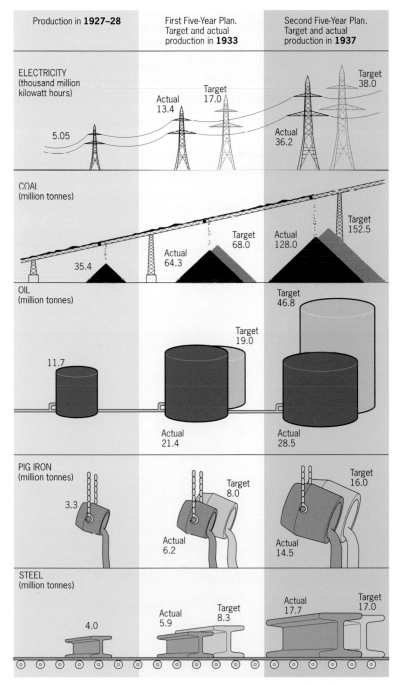

Target and actual production under the first two Five-Year Plans.

The consequences of the Five-Year Plans

- The main aim was achieved – by 1940, the USSR was in the 'first division' of industrial powers, along with Britain, Germany and the USA.
- Vast projects such as the Belomor Canal, the Dneiper Dam and the metalworks at Magnitogorsk were completed with amazing speed.
- Huge towns and factories were built from nothing, deep inside the USSR to protect them from invasion.
- Foreign technicians were brought in and enormous investment was put into education and training to produce skilled workers.
- Great pressure was put on workers to meet targets and to be 'Stakhanovites'. Stakhanov was a miner who managed to produce over 100 tonnes of coal in one shift, and was held up as a model to inspire all workers.
- The cost was high. Safety standards came second to meeting targets, discipline was harsh and many workers ended up in labour camps. All investment went into heavy industries – there were few consumer goods (clothes, luxuries).
- Millions of people were uprooted. As cities grew rapidly, as well as industrial sites, the supply of housing lagged behind demand. Many families lived together in one room.
- On the other hand, living conditions for some did gradually improve, especially families that were hailed as loyal Communists. Electricity became more common in cities. Education and hospital care were free.
- Russians could be proud of the impressive architecture that showed the triumphs of Communist society. For example, in Moscow the underground train system was built with huge spaces and bright paintings.
- The USSR was in a much better position to defend itself against its enemies – as was seen when Germany invaded in June 1941.

Comment

Alexei Stakhanov was given medals and treated as a hero. In fact, much of his achievement was exaggerated for propaganda purposes. He had assistants to help him, modern equipment, and was mining the best seam of coal.

Revision task

Draw up a table like the one below. Use the information and evidence in this section to complete it.

	Five-Year Plans	Collectivisation
Aims		
Methods		
Successes/failures		
Costs		

Exam practice

1 Explain the effects of collectivisation in the USSR in the 1930s. *(8 marks)*

2 'Stalin's Five-Year Plans in the years 1923–41 were a huge success for the USSR.' How far do you agree with this interpretation? Explain your answer. *(12 marks)*

Exam tip: q2 Exam practice question 2 on the left is a typical style of essay question used in the exams. First, prepare an answer in brief note form, jotting down reasons to agree and reasons to disagree. Then think how you can develop your ideas into longer arguments. Finally, consider what conclusion you might reach about the interpretation.

Key content

You need to have a good working knowledge of the following areas.
Tick off each item once you are confident in your knowledge.

- ❏ The death and funeral of Lenin; his *Testament*
- ❏ Stalin and Trotsky's claims to power and their policies
- ❏ Government, censorship and propaganda in the later 1920s
- ❏ The power struggle between Stalin and Trotsky and other rivals; why Stalin won
- ❏ Stalin's Communist Party dictatorship of the 1930s; the constitution of 1936
- ❏ The reasons for, extent of, and consequences of the purges and Great Terror
- ❏ The cult of personality
- ❏ Censorship; propaganda; secret police; labour camps
- ❏ The economic situation in the 1920s under the NEP; the need for change
- ❏ The theory, process and results of collectivisation
- ❏ The Five-Year Plans for industry
- ❏ The economic, political and social consequences of the plans

Check your knowledge online with our Quick quizzes at www.hodderplus.co.uk/modernworldhistory.

In 1929, the Nazis, led by Hitler, had only limited support in Germany. However, in the aftermath of the Wall Street Crash, the majority of Germans turned to extremist parties – the Communists or the Nazis. In January 1933, Hitler became Chancellor of Germany with the Nazis as the largest political party in the Reichstag. Quickly he increased his powers, declared himself Führer, and built up a dictatorship in Germany. Many Germans, especially at first, benefited from Nazi rule, with a more ordered society and fewer unemployed. Others, such as Communists and Jews, suffered. All suffered during the Second World War.

Key issues

As with all examination topics, you will be expected to do more than simply learn the content and write it out again. You will need to show understanding of key issues from the period. These are:

- How and why was Hitler able to become Chancellor in January 1933?
- How did Hitler change Germany from a democracy to a Nazi dictatorship, 1933–34, and then reinforce this?
- To what extent did Germans benefit from Nazi rule?

11.1 How and why was Hitler able to become Chancellor in January 1933?

The impact of the Wall Street Crash and the Depression

The recovery of the German economy was fragile. It depended heavily on American loans. In 1929, disaster struck with the Wall Street Crash.

- Many American banks were forced to recall their loans. German companies were unable to pay.
- German businesses began to close. Millions lost their jobs. By 1932, the number of unemployed had reached 6 million.
- Many became homeless as they could not afford to pay their rent or mortgage.
- More and more people felt let down by the Weimar Government and turned to extremist parties.

Cross reference

For detail on the background to the Wall Street Crash in the USA, see Chapter 9, pages 93–94. For details about the background in Germany, see Chapter 8.

Growth in support for the Nazis and other extremist parties

In the years 1929–33, as the effects of the Depression got worse, there was a rapid growth in support for extremist political parties. The Communists appealed to the poor working class. They held rallies, marches and meetings. The Communist Red Fighting League broke up meetings of political opponents, just like the Nazis did.

The Nazis tried to appeal to both workers and businessmen alike who had lost all their money and investments in the economic collapse.

- They spread their ideas effectively through Joseph Goebbels, the head of propaganda.
- Hitler's private army, the SA (the Brownshirts), caused trouble and violence at meetings run by their political opponents. The Nazis then blamed the Communists for causing the violence.
- Hitler's speeches concentrated on what was judged to be the most popular message. Usually this meant criticising the shameful Treaty of Versailles and the politicians who signed it, the rich Jews, and the Communists who were not interested in the German nationality.

The Weimar system of government and the failure of democracy

The Weimar Republic had had a difficult beginning after the First World War, but it had gained respectability in the later 1920s. Now it struggled to deal with the Depression.

Coalition governments were normal in Weimar Germany as the result of **proportional representation**. The President, the highly respected war hero General von Hindenburg, tried to create governments to solve the country's economic crisis. However, the result was a series of weak governments that did not command much loyalty from the German people as a whole.

Brüning was **Chancellor** between the 1930 and 1932 elections. He tried to deal with the crisis by raising taxes, cutting the salaries of government employees, and cutting the level of unemployment benefit. He became very unpopular. Many Germans believed that their democratic constitution was failing them. What was needed, they believed, was strong decisive government that would act firmly.

The Nazis gaining support, 1930–32

In the first year after the Wall Street Crash, it was the Communists and Socialists who benefited the most from economic chaos. This was seen in the Reichstag election in 1930. However, by 1932 the Nazi message had reached a large audience, with the Nazis being the largest party in the Reichstag after the July elections.

In 1932, there was a presidential election (held every seven years). Hitler stood against the elderly President Hindenburg, Although Hitler lost by 13 million votes to 19 million, he used the opportunity to put across the Nazi message of blaming the country's problems on the enemies of Germany (Jews, communists and foreign capitalists) and promising to build a stronger country.

He gained status in the eyes of many German citizens as a serious politician who would rescue Germany from the weak government from which it was suffering.

Presidential election result, 1932	
Candidate	Number of votes
Hindenburg	19 million
Hitler (Nazi)	13 million
Thälmann (Communist)	4 million

The elections of 1932

The July 1932 general election campaign was very violent. Nazis and Communists fought each other in street battles and nearly 100 people were killed.

The Nazis became the largest party in the Reichstag and Hitler demanded to be made Chancellor. However, Hindenburg was suspicious of Hitler and refused. Instead, he appointed Franz von Papen, a conservative politician with no party

> ### Key terms
>
> **Coalition:** the joining together of two or more political parties in a situation where no one political party gets a majority of the votes, in order to have sufficient support to pass laws.
>
> **Proportional representation:** a system in which the number of representatives from a given party is determined by how many votes that party gains nationally.
>
> **Chancellor:** chief minister (equivalent of Prime Minister in Britain).

base, as Chancellor. To achieve his aims, von Papen needed to increase his support in the Reichstag and so he called another election in November 1932. The Nazis lost seats but were still the largest party. Von Papen did not get the extra support he needed.

Party	Number of seats won in general election	
	July 1932	November 1932
Moderate parties		
Social Democrats	133	121
Centre Party	75	70
Extremists		
Communists (left wing)	89	100
Nazis (right wing)	230	196
Nationalists (right wing)	40	51

Hitler becomes Chancellor, January 1933

It was becoming increasingly clear that President Hindenburg could not continue to work with a Chancellor who did not have support in the Reichstag. Von Papen simply could not pass any of the measures he wanted.

- Hindenburg and von Papen decided to make Hitler Chancellor.
- They believed they would be able to control him once he was in power.
- On 30 January 1933, Hitler became German Chancellor and von Papen Vice-Chancellor.

Exam practice

1 Study **Source 1**. Explain why the Nazis were able to get more support during the years of the Depression (1930–32). *(8 marks)*

SOURCE 1

A view of the SA's activities in 1930. The cartoon was produced by the Social Democrats.

2 'Hitler became Chancellor of Germany because of the activities of the SA.' How far do you agree with this interpretation? Explain your answer. *(12 marks)*

> **Exam tip: q2** When faced with a question like this, first list the reasons why you might agree with the interpretation. Then think what other reasons help to explain why Hitler was able to become Chancellor. For a high mark and grade, you need to develop the reasons by giving details (fact and explanation) in your full answer.

11.2 How did Hitler change Germany from a democracy to a Nazi dictatorship, 1933–34, and then reinforce this?

SOURCE 2

Rudolph Diels, head of the Prussian (German) military police, explaining what he found at the police office in the Reichstag.

Marinus van der Lubbe was being questioned. He was smeared in dirt and sweating. He panted as if he had completed a tremendous task. There was a wild triumphant gleam in his eyes. He had Communist pamphlets in his pockets.

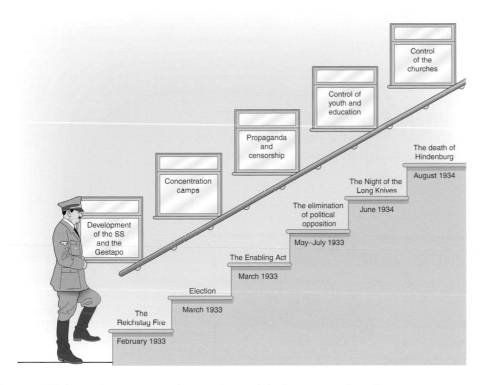

The route Hitler took to create a dictatorship and the formation of a police state.

The Reichstag Fire

During the election campaign, on the night of 27 February 1933, the Reichstag was burned to the ground. A Communist, Marinus van der Lubbe, was arrested for the crime. Hitler and the Nazis were able to exploit the fire for their own purposes.

- The Nazis were quick to blame the Communist Party.
- Hitler persuaded President Hindenburg to pass an emergency law restricting personal liberty.

The Reichstag Fire was a particularly important moment in the Nazis' rise to power. A key question here is whether the fire was staged by the Nazis.

Sources 2, 3 and 4 illustrate the problem of dealing with conflicting evidence. They suggest three possible explanations for the fire.

- Van der Lubbe acted alone.
- Van der Lubbe acted on behalf of the Communists.
- Nazi Stormtroopers (the SA) caused the fire, hoping to blame the Communists and win more support for Hitler in the general election.

The historian needs to consider each source carefully. Source 2 may be a primary source, but it is evidence from a Nazi police officer. Source 3 sounds balanced and confident, but where did Shirer get his evidence? Source 4 shows Hitler quickly taking the opportunity to spread anti-Communist propaganda.

SOURCE 3

William Shirer, an American writing about the Reichstag Fire in 1959, in his book *The Rise and Fall of the Third Reich*.

From Goering's palace an underground passage ran to the Reichstag building. Through this tunnel Karl Ernst, a former hotel porter who had become the leader of the Berlin SA, led his Stormtroopers. They scattered petrol and quickly returned to the palace. At the same time, van der Lubbe climbed in and set some fires of his own.

SOURCE 4

Adolf Hitler, 28 February 1933.

This act of arson is the most outrageous act yet committed by Communists in Germany. The burning of the Reichstag was to have been the signal for a bloody uprising and civil war.

The election of March 1933

As can be seen from the election results, the Nazis were the largest political party in the Reichstag in March 1933. However, Hitler was bitterly disappointed as the Nazis did not have an overall majority. They only had 44 per cent of the votes, and Hitler needed to pass laws legally.

However, he gained the support of the Nationalists who wanted to see Germany become a great country again. He also got support from the Centre Party by promising to protect the Catholic Church in Germany.

Main political parties	Seats won
Nazi Party	288
Nationalists (right wing)	52
Centre Party	74
Social Democrats (left wing)	120
Communists (extreme left wing)	81

In addition, by using the President's emergency law, the Communists were not allowed to take their seats in the Reichstag. To be totally sure of a high Nazi majority, when the Reichstag members assembled, heavily-armed SA men made their presence known.

SOURCE 5

"LET THE GERMAN PEOPLE DECIDE!"

The election of 6 March 1933. Above is a British cartoonist's view of what the election in Germany might be like. It appeared in a British newspaper on 1 March. Remember that the emergency decree following the Reichstag Fire had been announced the previous day. The notice on the polling booth reads 'Parties opposing Hitler are severely discouraged'.

Revision tasks

1 What do you think **Source 5** is saying about the election?
2 What techniques does the cartoonist use to get his message across?

The Enabling Act, March 1933

Hitler still did not have enough support to have complete control of Germany. An Enabling Act would give him the right to pass laws for the next four years without having to obtain the support of members in the Reichstag. However, to pass an Enabling Act Hitler needed to obtain the votes of two-thirds of Reichstag members, but he had the support of only just over half. This is what happened.

- Hitler ordered his SA to continue intimidating the opposition.
- The 81 Communist members of the Reichstag were expelled.
- In an atmosphere heavy with violence and threats, the Enabling Act was passed by 441 votes to 94.
- Hitler was given the power to rule for four years without consulting the Reichstag.

Comment

A vote of at least two-thirds in favour (rather than a simple majority) was needed because the Enabling Act involved a change in the constitution.

The elimination of political opposition

In July 1933, Hitler increased his grip on power even further. Using the powers of the Enabling Act, he outlawed all other parties and Germany became a one-party state. The democratic Weimar Republic had been destroyed and Germany had become a dictatorship.

Then Hitler turned on the trade unions.

- On 2 May 1933, Nazis broke into trade union offices all over the country and arrested thousands of trade union officials.
- Unions were banned and all workers became part of the German Labour Front.

The Night of the Long Knives

Once he had gained power, Hitler's priority was to rid himself of possible rivals. Ernst Röhm, leader of the SA, had played a major role in helping Hitler achieve power. However:

- The German army saw the SA as a rival – the army would not support Hitler unless the SA was disbanded.
- Some members of the SA looked to Hitler to follow a socialist programme of reform – Hitler was opposed to this since he knew he would lose the support of wealthy industrialists.
- Röhm was a threat to Hitler's dominance of the Nazi Party.

Hitler made a deal with the generals of the German army. They promised to support him as Commander-in-Chief of the armed forces if the SA was disbanded, and if he started a programme of rearmament. On 30 June 1934, SS assassination squads murdered Hitler's potential SA rivals, including Röhm (the SS was set up in 1925 as an elite section of the SA). It has been estimated that up to 400 people were killed in the 'Night of the Long Knives'.

The death of Hindenburg; Hitler becomes Führer

Just over one month later, President Hindenburg died. Hitler thereafter combined the posts of Chancellor and President and also became Commander-in-Chief of the armed forces. From this point onwards, soldiers swore personal allegiance to Hitler, who officially became known as *der Führer* (the leader).

Exam practice

1 Explain how Hitler was able to become a dictator by summer 1934. *(8 marks)*

Revision task

Make a copy of the following table. Use key words to complete each column to show how Hitler achieved his dictatorship.

	What Hitler did	Importance
The Reichstag Fire		
The Enabling Act		
The SA		

Exam tip For Exam practice question 1 above, you should aim to explain two or three factors (with some details) in order to reach the top level in the mark scheme.

One-party law and order

By the summer of 1933, Germany had become a one-party state. All other political parties had been banned. Anyone who openly criticised Hitler was imprisoned or worse. In theory, Hitler was all-powerful, making all decisions. However, in private, Hitler was very lazy and worked as little as possible, especially on details, which he left to those in command under him.

The SS and Gestapo

The police state that Hitler wanted was enforced ruthlessly by the SS (Hitler's bodyguard) and the **Gestapo**.

- They used terror tactics to intimidate, arrest and even kill any possible opponents.
- Enemies of the Nazis, such as liberals, socialists and Communists, were often arrested and sent to concentration camps without trial.

Key term

Gestapo: short for *Geheime Staatspolizei*, which means Secret State Police.

Concentration camps

The Gestapo could hold anyone arrested in 'protective custody' in a concentration camp. The camps were run by SS guards under the orders of the SS leader, Heinrich Himmler. Mostly they contained political prisoners. (The association of concentration camps with Jews came later, from 1939 onwards, during the Second World War.)

Propaganda and censorship

The main aim of propaganda was to provide the German people with a Nazi view of events. The other aim was to target certain groups, inside and outside Germany, who were seen as enemies – for example, Jews, Communists, socialists and liberals. The Minister of Propaganda, Goebbels, used his power to control all information that reached the German people.

- All newspapers were censored by the Government and allowed to print only stories favourable to the Nazis.
- Radio was controlled by the Government. Cheap radios were manufactured so that most Germans could afford one. Goebbels made sure that all radio plays, stories and news items were favourable to the Nazis.
- The Nazis took control of the German film industry. German films of the 1930s often showed great German heroes defeating their enemies. Cartoons were used to show Jews as weak and devious.
- Goebbels organised mass rallies. The most spectacular was held each August in Nuremberg. At the rallies, hundreds of thousands of Nazi supporters listened to choirs, sang songs and watched sporting events and firework displays.
- The Nazis used sporting events to spread their propaganda. The 1936 Berlin Olympic Games was used by the Nazis to suggest the superiority of the **Aryan race**.

Key term

Aryan race: the Nordic blond-haired, blue-eyed physical ideal of Nazi Germany. In practice, it became used as the Nazi term for non-Jewish Germans.

Control of education and youth movements

Teachers had to belong to the German Teachers' League and follow a Nazi curriculum.

- School textbooks were rewritten in support of Nazi ideas and history.
- Children were taught that the Aryan race was superior to others.
- Outside school, parents were encouraged to allow their children to join youth groups organised by the Nazis (for example, the Hitler Youth and the German Girls' League), where they were indoctrinated with Nazi ideas and beliefs.

Control of the Churches

In 1933, the Catholic Church in Germany signed an agreement (concordat) with Hitler. Both sides agreed not to interfere with each other. The Nazis, in effect, took over the Protestant churches in Germany under what was called the Reich Church. Many Protestants accepted this because they were Nazi supporters, even though many Christian elements of worship were not allowed.

> ## Revision task
> Use key words to explain how the following enabled the Nazis to maintain their dictatorship in the period 1933–39:
> - propaganda
> - the police state
> - control of the young.

The nature of continuing opposition and resistance in the Third Reich

Not everybody agreed with Hitler's policies. Many had gone along with his rule because of the good things he appeared to be achieving for Germany in the 1930s. Former political opponents were silenced. Many Communist Party members were arrested and many died in prison camps. Many went into exile abroad. Others held secret meetings, waiting for Hitler's popularity to decline. The churches in Germany did very little to oppose Hitler in the 1930s. Very few pastors were put in prison in the 1930s for speeches or actions against Nazi policies. Many pastors simply left Hitler's Reich Church (see page 112) and set up their own church. One leading opponent was Martin Niemöller, who was arrested in 1937 and spent the Second World War years in a concentration camp. Another was Dietrich Bonhoeffer, who openly preached that Nazism was anti-Christian. He was eventually arrested and executed in 1945.

By the late 1930s, for many Germans the benefits of Nazi rule were being outweighed by increasing unease at Nazi brutality – especially after persecution of the Jews reached a new height at Kristallnacht in November 1938. When war started in September 1939 with the invasion of Poland and then the invasion of the Netherlands, Belgium and France in spring 1940, some Germans started to move from opposition by words to opposition by actions.

> **Cross reference**
>
> *See page 116 for more on Kristallnacht.*

The White Rose Movement

Some students were appalled at the lack of opposition to Hitler and Nazi violence, especially when this became Europe-wide by 1941, and especially the terror being unleashed against the Jews. The White Rose group consisted of a small number of students at Munich University, led by Hans Scholl and his sister Sophie. They emphasised the importance of personal responsibility in questions of morality; the target audience was the educated middle class. They put up posters, handed out leaflets and scrawled anti-Nazi graffiti on walls. Hans and Sophie were arrested and tortured, before being beheaded in February 1943.

The Edelweiss Pirates

These were groups of teenagers, mostly of working-class origin, mainly active in the Rhineland and Ruhr areas, in opposition to the Hitler Youth. In particular, they tried to avoid conscription. These teenage rebel groups were not an organised movement, but the independent youth gangs that they created were seen as opposition to Nazi rule. The Nazis portrayed the 'pirates' as long-haired anti-social layabouts seeking to undermine Nazi achievements.

At first the Nazis arrested members and put them into labour camps. When this did not stop opposition, the Gestapo broke up Edelweiss groups and arrested the leaders in late 1942. Twelve were publicly hanged in Cologne in 1944.

However, the development of an anti-Nazi youth group, especially when mass bombing of German cities had started, showed the growing opposition to the ideals of a Nazi society.

The Kreisau Circle, 1939–44

Many educated, conservative Germans were increasingly opposed to the destruction that Hitler was causing in Europe. However, there was no united co-ordinated group. The nearest to this was the Kreisau Circle, a group of aristocrats, lawyers, churchmen and non-Nazi politicians, who met in secret from time to time at the home of Count Helmuth von Moltke. He was a Prussian landowner and a member of the aristocracy. He despised Hitler and criticised the atrocities being committed around Europe. The group was eventually broken up by the Gestapo. Moltke was arrested in January 1944 and shot in January 1945.

The Stauffenberg bomb plot, 1944

There were many plots against Hitler, most of them getting nowhere beyond outline plans. The plot in 1938 to blow up Hitler's plane with him on board failed because the bomb did not explode. The most famous plot – which had a good chance of success – was the Stauffenberg plot in 1944.

By 1944, many German officers were disillusioned with Hitler and the war. Claus von Stauffenberg had been a Nazi supporter in the 1930s because of his anti-Communist views. Now, with the war turning against Germany, his country was on the path to total ruin, and the brutality of the SS disgusted him. He led a plot to plant a bomb under a table at a meeting that Hitler was attending. Army officers would then seize power in Berlin. However, someone moved the briefcase containing the bomb slightly further away from Hitler. The bomb killed four people, but Hitler was only slightly injured. The conspirators were slow to act and confused when it became clear that Hitler had not been killed. All the plotters were rounded up and executed. Furthermore, Hitler used the plot as an excuse to arrest and execute all known opponents – more than 5,000 people.

> **Revision task**
> Why do you think there was so little opposition to Hitler, even during the Second World War? Write a paragraph to explain your view.

11.3 To what extent did Germans benefit from Nazi rule?

Economic policy – increased employment and self-sufficiency

Hitler had promised to remove unemployment. This was achieved by 1938 through a variety of policies.

- The Labour Service Corps was set up. From 1935, it was compulsory for all men aged 18–25 to serve in the Corps for six months.
- Unemployed men were used to build government-funded roads, motorways, houses, hospitals and schools.
- From 1935, all men aged 18–25 were compelled to do military service for two years.
- Rearmament provided thousands of jobs in arms factories and greatly boosted heavy industry.

Hitler was determined to make Germany self-sufficient. This was known as the policy of autarky.

- In 1934, Schacht was made Economics Minister. He tried to make Germany less dependent on imported raw materials and encouraged the growth of German industry.
- Schacht was later replaced by Goering, who brought in a Four-Year Plan for the economy. This set much higher targets for rearmament and tried to move Germany closer to autarky. Experiments were begun to produce artificial replacements for oil and rubber. These were not very successful.

Social policy

The Labour Front replaced trade unions. Workers were not allowed to leave their jobs without government permission, and strikes were made illegal. Opposition was rare. By the late 1930s, workers accepted the long working hours and lack of rights because they felt secure in their jobs, and many were pleased to see the German economy recovering.

The 'Strength Through Joy' movement organised leisure activities and provided the public with sports facilities, cheap holidays and entertainments. This movement also helped to plan the production of a 'people's car' (*Volkswagen*) that was cheap enough for many workers to afford. Many new motorways (autobahns) were built in the 1930s by those who had been unemployed.

Many Germans in the mid-1930s were pleased with the apparent improvements in their lives. Compared with the continuing economic depression in countries such as Britain and the USA, unemployment was falling rapidly and industry was expanding. Germans were regaining pride in their country. This was reinforced in 1936 when Germany hosted the Olympic Games in Berlin. With developing armed forces (which ignored the limits imposed by the Treaty of Versailles), Germans could feel pride in the re-occupation of the Rhineland (1936) and the union with Austria in March 1938 (see Chapter 3).

Effects of Nazi policy on women's lives

- Hitler stated that women's role was *Kinder, Küche, Kirche* (children, kitchen and the Church).
- In the Law for the Reduction of Unemployment, there were financial incentives for women to stay at home.
- The Nazis wanted to encourage as many births as possible of 'racially pure' children. There were financial incentives for this.
- The most productive mothers received special medals.
- German women who had held positions of responsibility before 1933 lost status. Female doctors and civil servants were sacked. From 1936, women could no longer be judges.
- There were campaigns to direct how women should dress and look – for example, hair should be worn in plaits or a bun, and make-up should not be worn.
- On the other hand, women who were happy to be mothers and remained loyal to their Führer were very happy with their lifestyle.

Effects of Nazi policy on German culture

German culture was restricted. Only drama, films, music and art that glorified the Nazis was allowed. Anything that was seen as decadent was banned. Jewish writers and composers were banned, and Jewish intellectuals lost their university positions. Some scientists emigrated – for example, Albert Einstein, who later helped to develop the nuclear bomb in the USA.

Racial persecution – the Jews

Although all opponents of the Nazi regime were persecuted, it was the Jews who received the worst treatment of all.

In 1933, the Nazis organised a boycott of all Jewish businesses, doctors, dentists, and so on. Jewish shops were marked with the star of David and the word '*Jude*'.

In education, Jewish children were intimidated at school and Germans were taught that Jews were unclean and responsible for Germany's defeat in the First World War.

In 1935, the Nuremberg Laws were introduced in Germany. Under these laws:

- Jews could no longer be German citizens
- marriages between Jews and Aryans were forbidden
- Jews had to wear a yellow star on their clothing.

Kristallnacht

It is not clear how much most Germans knew about the persecution. However, in 1938 an event occurred that left nobody in any doubt.

In early November 1938, a Polish Jew, Herschel Grynszpan, shot a German diplomat in Paris. Hitler ordered an immediate attack on Jews and their property in Germany. Between 9 and 10 November, thousands of Jewish businesses were attacked and 200 synagogues burned down. This was called *Kristallnacht*, 'The Night of Broken Glass'.

Violence against Jews in Germany increased. Himmler, head of the SS, began to expand the plans for building concentration camps.

Sources 6 and 7 give two differing views about *Kristallnacht*. The key question to be answered is, which source gives the more reliable view of the events of 9 November 1938?

As with other sources we have examined, the test for reliability depends particularly upon who wrote the source and why he or she wrote it. Source 6 gives a Nazi view of events and we have little reason to trust what it says. Source 7 is probably a more reliable view of events and it is supported by our background knowledge. However, Source 7 would be more useful (and we could be more sure about its reliability) if we knew who the observer was, and from where he or she had observed the events described. In this way, we would be able to cross-check this description with other evidence.

Persecution of other groups within Nazi society

Gypsies had long been viewed with suspicion and hatred because of their different lifestyle. The Nuremberg Laws were used against them. Other homeless people were also rounded up and put to forced labour.

The Nazi attitude towards those who suffered mental or physical problems was even worse. Hitler wanted to create a master race of superior Aryans. Any Germans who suffered from disabilities had to be sterilised so that they did not pass on less-than-perfect genes. By the end of the 1930s, a policy had started of mercy killing those who did not measure up to the Aryan ideal.

The Final Solution

Once war started in 1939 the plight of the Jews became desperate, especially in countries such as Poland that were conquered by the Nazis. Impossible living conditions existed for Jews in cities such as Warsaw. Also in 1941, the Nazis captured large parts of the USSR which contained millions of Jews. 'Shooting parties' of special SS units rounded up Jews (and other undesirables such as Communists) and shot them.

The next stage was when, in the summer of 1941, Goering ordered Himmler (head of the SS) and Heydrich (an SS general) to carry out 'the final solution'. In January 1942, Nazi leaders held a conference to discuss the most efficient method of destroying a race of people. Death camps, which had good rail networks, were built in eastern Europe. By the end of the war more than 1 million Jews had been killed in the gas chambers at Auschwitz. At least 2 million more Jews were killed in other death camps. Many more perished as a result of terrible conditions in concentration camps and ghettos. Altogether about 6 million Jews had died by 1945.

SOURCE 6

Nazi press statement, 10 November 1938.

It was a spontaneous wave of anger throughout Germany as a result of the cowardly murder of Third Secretary von Rath in the German Embassy in Paris.

SOURCE 7

An American observer, 1938.

The damage was done by SS men and Stormtroopers not in uniform, each group having been provided with hammers, axes, crowbars and incendiary bombs.

Revision task

Describe the Nuremberg Laws and their effects on Jews.

Exam practice

1 'German people in the 1930s benefited from Nazi rule.' How far do you agree with this interpretation? Explain your answer.

(12 marks)

Exam tip Draw up two lists to answer Exam practice question 1 above – the benefits and the losses for the German people. Think about what 'German people' means here. Which people were increasingly excluded in the 1930s? Try to link the benefits and losses with different groups of people. If you were writing a full essay, you might also consider whether the benefits were equally spread for these groups in the years 1933–45.

The effect of the war on the civilian population

At first, the civilian population did not suffer much. Indeed, some goods became plentiful as they were brought back home from conquered countries. However, as soon as the Allies began to counter-attack, German civilians suffered very badly.

1. Bombing

Air raids on German cities began as early as 1940. From 1942 onwards they became more frequent and heavier. Many Germans left the cities to join relatives in the countryside. Hitler Youth helped to organise the evacuation of children, separated from their parents.

The bombing destroyed factories and transport systems, thus contributing to more problems of shortages of food and materials.

In March 1942, the RAF started major bombing raids, in conjunction with the US Air Force. By 1943, 43 German cities were being repeatedly bombed. The highest concentration of raids to attack Germany's main industries was on cities in the Rhineland and Ruhr areas. Official reports spoke of the civilian population remaining calm. Personal accounts after the war provide a rather different picture of the terrifying ordeal.

Goebbels attempted to keep up morale as the air raids got worse by talking of new lethal weapons that were going to be launched at the enemy. But 2 million homes had been destroyed; many were homeless; and the many nights of disrupted sleep led to much exhaustion.

SOURCE 8

	On Germany	On Britain
1940	10,000	36,844
1941	30,000	21,858
1942	40,000	3,260
1943	120,000	2,298
1944	650,000	9,151
1945	500,000	761

The amount of bombing (in tons) on Britain and Germany.

2. Rationing

It was difficult to keep up morale once rationing started, but the Nazis were determined to make sure that shortages never reached a critical level. Rationing was introduced immediately after the war started, with rations based on age, occupation and racial origin. As long as the USSR was an ally (under the Nazi-Soviet Pact of August 1939), some supplies such as grain could be imported from there. After summer 1941, shortages became more common, but were not as bad as they had been in the First World War. However, by 1945 levels were critical in terms of food and fuel in many German cities.

3. Propaganda

In the first two years of the war it was easy to keep morale at a high level. German armed forces seemed to be achieving victory after victory. The invasion of the USSR in June 1941 was seen as a crusade against Communism and the Slav races of eastern Europe. The Nazis appealed to German patriotism. Women were encouraged to help solve the labour shortage by going to work – particularly in war industries and transport. Posters encouraged Germans to use less coal and to look out for Communist spies.

However, when the USSR had not been defeated by December 1941 and German casualties were mounting rapidly, the mood quickly worsened. Many Germans were becoming cynical about German propaganda, and this increased near the end of 1942 with the news of major setbacks. The German Sixth Army had been surrounded at Stalingrad by Soviet forces, and the Germans and Italians had been defeated in North Africa at the Battle of El Alamein.

By 1944 war weariness was growing and the loyalty of many Germans was growing thin. No amount of propaganda could counteract the devastating effects of the aerial bombardments and most Germans could see that the war was being lost.

The D-Day landings of June 1944 led to the liberation of France and by early 1945 the invasion of Germany itself.

	1940	1941	1942	1943	1944
Coal production (million tonnes)	269	315	318	340	348
Tank production	2,200	5,200	9,200	17,300	22,100
Aircraft production	10,200	11,800	15,400	24,800	39,800

German war production 1940–44.

The effect of the war on the German economy

- In the early years, German industries that contributed to the war effort thrived. Women were encouraged to fill the gaps in the labour force. Help with materials and food was provided by the USSR until the German invasion of June 1941. Conquered territories such as Romania and Sweden were important for providing metals.
- British and American bombing targeted cities and, in particular, industrial centres and rail and road networks with increasing numbers of bombs.
- From 1943 when 'total war' was declared by the Nazis, all industrial production was geared towards the war effort, leading to acute shortages in other commodities.
- However, allied bombing destroyed much of the fuel supplies, which were essential for industrial production.
- In late 1944, more than 200,000 men were tied up in repairing electricity, oil and gas supplies.
- In 1944–45, tank production, at a time when increased production was the priority, actually fell by 35 per cent. After the end of the war industrial output was only one-third of the 1938 level.
- By early 1945, with the invasion of German territory, morale was rock-bottom. In the cities living standards were terrible. More than 20 million Germans were homeless, with 20 per cent of all housing destroyed. More than 3 million civilians had been killed.
- The German economy, totally devoted to a war that was being lost, was in ruins. When the Russians, Americans, British and French took control of parts of Berlin, a total rebuilding programme was needed – for houses and for industry – and major repairs to all pipework for providing water, sewage, electricity and gas. In 1946–47 living conditions actually became worse. The German economy was in ruins and it is estimated that nearly half of all 'sales' were carried out by bartering.

Exam practice

1 Explain how German civilians were affected by the Second World War. *(8 marks)*

2 Explain why the German economy was able to expand in the early years of the war and why this was not sustained in 1944–45. *(8 marks)*

Exam tip With Exam practice questions 1 and 2 above, you should provide details that include some precise information for the top level of marks.

Key content

You need to have a good working knowledge of the following areas.
Tick off each item once you are confident in your knowledge.

- ❏ The effects of the Wall Street Crash on Germany; the Depression
- ❏ The growth in support for Nazis and other extremist parties, 1929–1932
- ❏ The problems with the Weimar system of government; the elections of 1930 and 1932
- ❏ Hitler's invitation to become Chancellor in January 1933; reactions of the German people
- ❏ The Reichstag Fire; the election of March 1933; the Enabling Act
- ❏ Continuing opposition and resistance: the White Rose Movement, the Edelweiss Pirates, The Kreisau Circle, the Stauffenberg bomb plot, 1944
- ❏ Getting rid of political opposition: banning other political parties and trade unions
- ❏ The Night of the Long Knives; the death of Hindenburg; Hitler becomes Führer
- ❏ The SS and Gestapo; concentration camps
- ❏ Propaganda; censorship; control of the media, education, youth movements and churches
- ❏ Continuing opposition and resistance: the White Rose Movement, the Edelweiss Pirates, the Kreisau Circle, the Stauffenberg bomb plot, 1944
- ❏ Getting rid of unemployment; self-sufficiency
- ❏ The effects of Nazi policies on the lives of Germans, including on women and on culture
- ❏ The persecution of the Jews and other non-Aryan groups such as the Gypsies; the Final Solution

Check your knowledge online with our Quick quizzes at www.hodderplus.co.uk/modernworldhistory.

Chapter 12: Depression and the New Deal: USA, 1929–1941

Following the Wall Street Crash in October 1929, the USA experienced a huge economic depression. Many businesses went bankrupt, millions became unemployed, and many more lost their homes as they could not afford mortgage payments. President Hoover was unsuccessful in solving the problems and was replaced by Franklin Roosevelt in 1933. He introduced what he called a New Deal, which helped the USA to start an economic recovery. However, even in the late 1930s the country still faced major problems. It was the outbreak of the Second World War that led to huge demands on industry and manpower.

Key issues

As with all examination topics, you will be expected to do more than simply learn the content and write it out again. You will need to show understanding of key issues from the period. These are:

- How serious were the effects of the Depression on the American people?
- How did Roosevelt deal with the Depression?
- How far was the New Deal successful in ending the Depression in the USA?

12.1 How serious were the effects of the Depression on the American people?

The effects of the Wall Street Crash

- Over 100,000 companies went bankrupt by 1933.
- Many banks ceased to exist as they could not pay back investors.
- By 1933, there were 14 million unemployed. Some industries and businesses were hit worse than others – for example, car production was reduced by 80 per cent. Industrial workers and African Americans usually suffered most.
- For those in work, wages were often reduced – for example, in the manufacturing industries wages were cut by an average of 20 per cent.
- Farmers suffered badly. Incomes dropped by more than half between 1929 and 1933 and many were forced to sell their land.
- Many farm workers who did not own any land lost their jobs and were forced to travel around looking for work.
- Unemployment often led to failure to pay mortgages and banks repossessing homes. Many homeless people wandered the streets and slept on park benches. Unplanned camps were set up on the edge of towns and cities, which came to be known as 'Hoovervilles'.
- Soup kitchens were set up in cities such as New York.
- Local relief programmes could not cope with demand. (There was no national social security system or unemployment benefit in the USA.)

Cross reference

For further details on the effects of the Wall Street Crash, as well as a description of what happened, see Chapter 9, pages 93–95.

Hoover's attempts to deal with the Depression

Most Americans blamed President Hoover for the crash. Hoover insisted that the situation was not too serious, and that 'prosperity is just around the corner'. This unfounded optimism upset many Americans.

In some ways, Hoover was criticised unfairly. He did take action between 1929 and 1933. For example, he:

- set up the Reconstruction Finance Corporation (RFC), which lent money to banks, industries and agriculture
- tried to encourage American exports (without much success)
- started to build the Hoover Dam on the Colorado River, which created jobs
- cut taxes so that people had more to spend
- provided $300 million in 1932 to individual states to help unemployed people.

Overall, however, he still believed in **rugged individualism** and showed little real sympathy for the poor. By the time of the 1932 presidential election campaign, the US economy was showing no real signs of recovery.

Revision task
List the reasons that you can find on this page to support **Source 1**.

Key term

Rugged individualism: the notion that people should overcome problems and succeed by their own efforts and hard work, not by receiving help from the Government.

The hungry and homeless queue for Christmas dinner outside the Municipal Lodging House, New York, 25 December 1931.

The unpopularity of Hoover

Hoover had become very unpopular with many Americans by 1932. This was partly unfair. There had never been a similar crisis on this scale, and Hoover's Government was ill-prepared to deal with it. Many American businessmen at the time believed that balancing the budget was the most important thing; borrowing a lot would be reckless. Therefore, they believed, Hoover's cautious approach would bring the USA out of the Depression. However, the unemployed, the poverty-stricken, the hungry and the homeless were not interested in eventual recovery. They wanted action with immediate results.

The episode of the bonus marchers in 1931 made Hoover's reputation worse.

- Soldiers who had fought in the First World War and suffered disabilities were being paid an annual pension.
- In addition, it had been agreed that they should be paid an extra sum – a bonus – in 1945. With the Depression hitting many of them badly, 20,000 of these soldiers and their families marched to Washington and demanded their bonus payments to be paid immediately.

- They squatted outside the White House. The President feared that there would be violence, and the army forcibly removed them.
- There were many injuries and two babies died from the effects of the tear gas that was used to disperse them.

Roosevelt's election campaign

Franklin D. Roosevelt was very different in character from President Hoover. He had been born into a wealthy family, was well-educated, became a lawyer and then a Senator. However, in the early 1920s he contracted polio, which left him with weak legs. For much of the time he had to be in a wheelchair. In spite of this, he was determined to re-enter politics. He became Governor of New York State in 1928. As State Governor during the Depression, he gained a reputation for action.

During the presidential election in 1932, he promised:

- government schemes to provide more jobs
- action to help industry and agriculture
- help for the poor and unemployed
- the end of prohibition.

He was a good speaker and impressed many people with his outgoing character and determination, especially as he was coping with the effects of polio. People tended not to notice that there was very little detail provided in his promises.

Roosevelt wins the election, November 1932

Roosevelt won the election by a large margin, winning in 42 of the 48 states. However, many people voted for Hoover, who still had the support of many powerful people and interest groups who wanted to see a return to life as it had been for the rich in the 1920s.

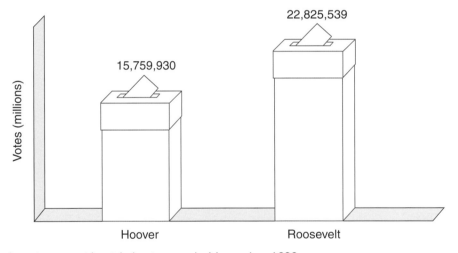

The American presidential election result, November 1932.

SOURCE 2

Frances Perkins, the first female member of Roosevelt's Government, wrote about the campaign. From *Time* magazine, 6 April 1970.

A newcomer in the national field, Roosevelt had to get out and become known. He saw thousands of Americans. He liked going around the countryside. His personal relationship with crowds was on a warm, simple level of friendly, neighbourly exchange of affection.

Exam practice

1 Explain why F. D. Roosevelt won the presidential election in 1932. *(8 marks)*

Revision task

Draw up a two-column table to summarise, in your own words, why Roosevelt won the 1932 election.

Reasons for Hoover's unpopularity	Reasons for Roosevelt's popularity

Exam tip For Exam practice question 1 above, you should aim to explain two or three reasons (with some details) in order to reach the top level in the mark scheme. If you have done the revision task on the left you will already have plenty of ideas to use in your answer.

12.2 How did Roosevelt deal with the Depression?

Roosevelt's fireside chats

On the day that Roosevelt became President in March 1933, he spoke boldly to the American people:

'So first of all let me assert my firm belief that the only thing we have to fear is fear itself – nameless, unreasoning, unjustified terror, which paralyses needed efforts to convert retreat into advance … Our greatest primary task is to put people to work. This is no unsolvable problem if we face it wisely and courageously.'

Eight days later, he gave the first of what became known as his 'fireside chats' – radio broadcasts to the American people. He spoke in a simple and friendly way, and gained enthusiastic support from many Americans who were not used to this direct approach. It was particularly important to gain public confidence at this time because of the banking crisis, which had to be solved before anything else could be achieved.

Later in the same month, Roosevelt brought prohibition to an end. The brewing of beer and the manufacture of other alcoholic drinks was legal again. This was seen as an important indication that there was a change of direction in government.

The banking crisis

Americans had little confidence in the banks. Many Americans had withdrawn their savings, leading to many banks going out of business. If more Americans tried to withdraw their money, the whole banking system would collapse.

The Government declared a 'bank holiday' and closed all banks. It officially backed 5,000 banks and reassured the American people that their money was safe, restoring confidence in the banking system when these approved banks reopened a few days later.

> **Comment**
>
> *Technically, Roosevelt's actions to deal with the banking crisis are not part of the New Deal, though they are often treated as such.*

SOURCE 3

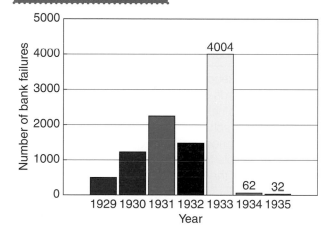

Bank failures, 1929–35.

SOURCE 4

A cartoon dated 3 March 1933, showing President Roosevelt throwing out the policies of the previous government.

Revision task

What can you learn about the New Deal from **Sources 3** and **4** above?

The New Deal

Roosevelt promised action – though he did not have a clear idea of exactly what should be done. He employed a panel of experts who became known as the Brains Trust. These people put together a programme of ideas. This was called the New Deal. The New Deal Programme had three main aims:

1 Relief – relieving extreme poverty, feeding the starving, and providing shelter for the homeless
2 Recovery – reviving the economy by getting industry going and people working
3 Reform – increasing the responsibilities of government by helping those in need in society such as the sick, disabled and old.

The First 'Hundred Days'

The economy was in such a bad state that **Congress** was willing to pass a lot of laws quickly. This period is known as the first 'Hundred Days' when thirteen major new laws were passed. The main ones are summarised below:

> **Key term**
>
> **Congress:** the American representative assemblies (the equivalent of Parliament in Britain). There are two houses, the Senate and the House of Representatives. Roosevelt had majority Democrat support in both houses.

Hundred Days legislation, 9 March–16 June 1933		
Legislation	Problem	Action
Federal Emergency Relief Administration (FERA)	Poverty and unemployment	500 million dollars allocated to help relieve suffering of poor (food, clothing, etc.); seed and equipment for farmers; schemes to create jobs.
Civilian Conservation Corps (CCC)	Unemployment among young men	Men aged 18–25 given six months' work. Had to send most of their pay home to parents/wives. About 300,000 joined in 1933; by 1940, there were 2 million.
Public Works Administration (PWA) (became Works Progress Administration in 1935)	Unemployment	Paid for public works projects (for example, schools, roads, hospitals) and used unemployed workers.
Agricultural Adjustment Administration (AAA)	Rural poverty, unemployment and low crop prices	Advised farmers on marketing and farming techniques and helped solve problem of overproduction by government buying up produce. Farmers became more organised but wealthy farmers gained most.
National Industrial Recovery Act (NIRA)	General economic condition of the USA	Set up National Recovery Administration (NRA), which set standards on working practices (hours, child labour). This helped create more jobs. Employers in the scheme displayed the eagle symbol of government approval and the Government encouraged people to use these firms. Over 2 million employers joined the scheme.
Tennessee Valley Authority (TVA)	Agricultural overproduction and regular flooding had ruined livelihoods of farm workers in Tennessee Valley. No alternative jobs in industry. Area covered parts of six states and was too big for any one state to deal with.	Huge public works projects: dams, irrigation, canals and water transport. Hydroelectric power created thousands of jobs. Farmers given loans and training in soil conservation. New housing built.

Other New Deal legislation

More laws continued to be passed in the next few years. Some were updating existing laws; some were entirely new.

Civilian Works Administration (CWA), November 1933

This provided temporary work for 4 million people during Roosevelt's first winter as President (1933–34). This was a lifesaver for many.

National Recovery Administration (NRA), 1933

This set out to improve working conditions in industry by setting out fair wages and establishing workers' rights to join a trade union. Industries were encouraged to set up a code of fair practice – and many did. However, in 1935, the Supreme Court declared the NRA to be unlawful. The Wagner Act of 1935 re-established some of what had been lost.

Home Owners Loan Corporation (HOLC), 1933

This gave out loans to homebuyers with low mortgages. The aim was to encourage home ownership and avoid owners having to surrender their home because they were behind with mortgage payments.

Works Progress Administration (WPA), 1935

This replaced the PWA. It extended the range of employment provided, from building work to the Federal Theatre Project, which gave work to unemployed artists and writers.

Social Security Act, 1935

This provided federal aid for the elderly and set up an unemployment insurance scheme. However, the provisions were far less comprehensive than in Germany or Britain. The pension payments were not due to start until 1940, and the unemployment benefit was only a small amount for a maximum of sixteen weeks.

To people at the time, the New Deal was extraordinary. No government had ever played such a large role in the lives of ordinary Americans. The key question on this topic is therefore: was the New Deal an American social and economic revolution? Historians disagree, as Sources 5 and 6 show.

Cross reference

See pages 126–7 for details of the actions of the Supreme Court.

Exam practice

1 Explain how the New Deal tried to provide 'relief'. *(8 marks)*

Exam tip For Exam practice question 1 above, you should aim to explain two or three factors (with some details) in order to reach the top level in the mark scheme.

SOURCE 5

Historian Carl Degler, 1959.

The conclusion seems inescapable that the New Deal was a revolutionary response to a revolutionary situation.

SOURCE 6

Historian Barton J. Bernstein, 1969.

The New Deal was neither a third American Revolution as Carl Degler suggests, nor even a half-way revolution.

Revision tasks

1 The New Deal was intended to cover three aims, as shown in the table below. Look back over the details of the New Deal and fill in brief details for each New Deal Act in the relevant column.

Relief	Recovery	Reform

2 Study **Sources 5** and **6**. They disagree about the New Deal. Draw up a table like the one below to list evidence to support each opinion.

Reasons to support Source 5	Reasons to support Source 6

12.3 How far was the New Deal successful in ending the Depression in the USA?

The Second New Deal

Between 1933 and 1935 there was a great deal of activity, with many laws being passed. Roosevelt was keen to keep the momentum going, and some of his later laws, from 1935 onwards, have been called the 'Second New Deal'. These were often passed in response to criticism he was receiving and, increasingly, they were concerned with working and living conditions and reforming society.

However, the extent of recovery was always limited, because as soon as government spending slackened in 1937 unemployment shot up again.

How effective was the New Deal in achieving its aims?

On a personal level, Roosevelt was hugely successful. He was elected four times as president. In 1936, he won by a huge landslide – winning all but two of the 48 states and gaining over 27 million votes, the highest number ever received up to that time. He managed to appeal to people's sense of belonging as American citizens, and made them feel that he understood their problems.

Criticisms and opposition to the New Deal

The result of the 1936 election showed that the majority of people supported Roosevelt. However, over 16 million people had voted against him. Many people, for a variety of reasons, criticised his policies.

Business leaders

They were unhappy about various aspects of the New Deal:
- regulations on working conditions
- the growth of trade unions and their increasing power
- the huge cost of the welfare programmes (which came from taxes paid by Americans).

The states

Some states were concerned about the New Deal because:
- measures like the TVA cut right across the rights of individual states
- they feared that the Federal Government was becoming too powerful.

Politicians

Some politicians opposed the New Deal.
- Republicans (not surprisingly) bitterly opposed the Democrat Roosevelt. They thought he was making the Government too powerful and quashing the traditional reliance on self-help.
- Even some conservative Democrats opposed him.
- Some radicals in the USA, like Huey Long, believed the New Deal did not go far enough. Another critic, Father Coughlin, a Catholic priest, broadcast his ideas on Sunday evening radio to over 40 million people. He criticised Roosevelt for not doing enough to help the poor.

The Supreme Court

The Supreme Court clashed with Roosevelt.
- Its judges (mainly old and Republican) ruled that several of the New Deal measures were illegal. For example, they argued that the Constitution did not

> **Comment**
>
> *The term 'Second New Deal' can be a little confusing. It is usually used to describe some of Roosevelt's later measures, both before and after his re-election in 1936. The emphasis in these was on social concerns rather than the economy as a whole. When a question refers to the New Deal, consider all the measures.*

allow a president to control businesses. They said that the rights of individual states were being lost to the increasing power of Federal Government.
- Matters came to a head in 1937 when Roosevelt wanted to appoint six new judges to alter the political balance of the Court in favour of the Democrats. This plan failed but afterwards Supreme Court opposition lessened.

How effective was the New Deal in achieving its aims?

Below is a summary of its main weaknesses and strengths.

Weaknesses

- When Roosevelt cut back his programmes in 1937, unemployment shot up.
- He never fully conquered unemployment in the 1930s; it was only solved by the USA's entry into the Second World War in 1941.
- The USA's trade (and the world's trade) did not recover.
- He failed to convince even his own supporters to change the organisation of the Supreme Court to stop it opposing his reforms.
- African Americans gained relatively little from the New Deal.

Successes

- In the USA, the Depression did not lead to extreme movements like Communism or Nazism taking hold. Roosevelt restored Americans' faith in democracy.
- Many millions of jobs were created and vital relief (food, shelter, clothing) was supplied to the poor.

Historians and others at the time argued about the success or failure of the New Deal. Sources 7 and 8 give two contrasting views expressed in the 1930s.

SOURCE 7

Letter sent to President Roosevelt in the 1930s.

Dear Mr President,
This is just to tell you everything is alright now. The man you sent found our house alright and we went down to the bank with him and the mortgage can go on for a while longer. You remember I wrote to you about losing the furniture too. Well, your man got it back for us. I never heard of a president like you, Mr Roosevelt. Mrs — and I are old folks and don't amount to much, but we are joined with millions of others in praying for you every night. God bless you Mr Roosevelt.

SOURCE 8

R. Shaw, *The New Deal – Its Unsound Theories and Irreconcilable Policies*, 1935.

The New Deal is nothing more or less than an effort to take away from the thrifty what the thrifty and their ancestors have accumulated, and give it to others who have not earned it, or whose ancestors haven't earned it for them, and never would have earned it and never will earn it.

As historians, we have to take care in using these sources, for several reasons.
- Neither source is attempting to balance the successes and failures of the New Deal – each represents a single view.
- Each source could be a 'one-off'. We do not know how many letters like Source 7 Roosevelt received, and we are not sure how many people agreed with the views expressed in it. However, our knowledge of the period does help, because we know millions voted for Roosevelt.
- As for Source 8, the title of the book from which this source has been taken is in itself an attack on the New Deal. It indicates the biased nature of the writer's argument.

The impact of the Second World War on American economic recovery, 1939–41

The USA officially remained neutral from September 1939 to December 1941, but Roosevelt's Government was increasingly drawn into the war.

- In 1940, Congress allowed Britain and other countries to buy weapons and other goods on a 'cash and carry' basis.
- In March 1941, Congress agreed to a Lend Lease programme, which allowed the USA to ship large quantities of materials to Britain.

As a result of these measures, in these years the US economy quickly recovered. This was even more pronounced when the USA declared war in December 1941 after the bombing of Pearl Harbor. The US economy doubled in production levels between 1938 and 1944. Unemployment disappeared with millions of men and women employed in industries and millions more in the armed forces.

The Depression was a thing of the past. The New Deal had started the recovery of the economy, and the USA's involvement in the Second World War completed the process. It also marked the emergence of the USA as a fully involved world power, keen to play a major role in world affairs.

Revision task

Divide a page into two columns. In one column, list what you see as the five main achievements of the New Deal. In the other, list five things that suggest that the New Deal had very limited success.

Then write a paragraph explaining your overall view of how far the New Deal ended the Depression.

Exam practice

1 'The New Deal failed to achieve its three main aims.' How far do you agree with this interpretation? Explain your answer.

(12 marks)

Exam tip Exam practice question 1 above is a typical style of essay question used in the exams. First, prepare an answer in brief note form, jotting down reasons to agree and reasons to disagree. Then think how you can develop your ideas into longer arguments. Finally, consider what conclusion you might reach about the interpretation.

Key content

You need to have a good working knowledge of the following areas.
Tick off each item once you are confident in your knowledge.

- ❏ The effects of the Wall Street Crash and Depression on the American people
- ❏ The collapse of business and industry; unemployment and its effects
- ❏ Hoover's attempts to deal with the Depression; economic failure
- ❏ The unpopularity of Hoover and the election of Roosevelt
- ❏ Roosevelt as President: fireside chats; the banking crisis; the New Deal's aims
- ❏ The main Alphabet Agencies: AAA, FERA, CWA, PWA, WPA, CCC, TVA
- ❏ The New Deal helping industry; the NRA
- ❏ The New Deal's social programme : the HOLC and the Social Security Act
- ❏ How far the New Deal achieved its aims; the Second New Deal
- ❏ Criticism and opposition to the New Deal – the Supreme Court and politicians
- ❏ The US attitude to the Second World War; Lend Lease policy; increase in US exports
- ❏ US economic recovery, 1939–1941

Check your knowledge online with our Quick quizzes at www.hodderplus.co.uk/modernworldhistory.

After the Second World War, most African Americans were treated as second-class citizens. They suffered discrimination in law and in their everyday treatment by many white Americans. However, with the actions of Rosa Parks, the courage of nine black students at Little Rock High School, and the help of decisions by the Supreme Court, the legal situation changed significantly.

Martin Luther King was the most famous name among those leading the demands for change, but even he found it difficult to change people's attitudes. His dream of peaceful non-violent methods was at odds with the violence that occurred between white police and African American demonstrators and also in race riots in cities such as Los Angeles. When King was assassinated in 1968, many African Americans still lagged behind average American standards of living and levels of education.

Cross reference

For more about the background of racial segregation, see Chapter 9, page 91.

Key issues

As with all examination topics, you will be expected to do more than simply learn the content and write it out again. You will need to show understanding of key issues from the period. These are:

- To what extent did racial inequality exist in the USA after the Second World War?
- How effective were the methods used by members of the civil rights movement between 1961 and 1968?
- How important was Martin Luther King in the fight for civil rights in the USA?

13.1 To what extent did racial inequality exist in the USA after the Second World War?

African American soldiers' experience of war

After the Japanese attack on Pearl Harbor in December 1941, the USA was at war. What happened in the next four years had a huge effect on race relations in the USA.

- With hugely increased demand for production from war industries, over 2 million African Americans migrated north to industrial cities. This led to tensions between white and black Americans in cities such as Detroit, with competition for housing leading to race riots.
- Gradually, black and white Americans found themselves working side by side in factories, but not always in harmony.
- African Americans became more aware of their unequal status in society, and saw the possibility of change. Demand for their labour gave them greater bargaining power for better wages and working conditions. The activities in some cities of

sit-ins and boycotts anticipated the large-scale protests that developed in the late 1950s. There was little change, however, in the southern states of the USA.

- Over 1 million African Americans served in the armed forces, mostly in segregated regiments, and often with white officers. After the war, African American returning soldiers questioned their segregation, having fought for the same cause of freedom. This was made worse by the difficulty they faced in finding jobs when competing with white ex-soldiers.

Segregation in the southern states after 1945

In the southern states of the USA, laws had been passed that enforced the **segregation** (or separation) of white and African Americans, and ensured that African Americans were seen as inferior to white Americans. These laws had been passed in the late nineteenth century, and their attitudes had been reinforced in the first half of the twentieth century. These so-called **Jim Crow** laws, passed by many southern states, imposed racial segregation in every aspect of life – for example, education, transport and housing.

Many African Americans had migrated to the northern industrial cities where they could find jobs, but even here they were poorly paid and poorly housed. African American ghettos grew up in parts of some cities such as New York. The only difference for African Americans in the north was that some were able to escape their poverty and isolation through sport or music such as jazz.

In the Second World War, many African Americans had fought and worked alongside white Americans. It was not a surprise, therefore, that some African Americans began to challenge the Jim Crow laws. In the short term, this encouraged many white Americans to tighten up existing laws still further in order to protect their privileged positions in society.

Ku Klux Klan

This organisation was originally founded in 1866 after the American Civil War. Its purpose was to make sure that African Americans, now free from slavery, still remained socially inferior to white Americans. In the 1920s, the Klan had a resurgence of support.

After the Second World War, when some African Americans were openly questioning laws that discriminated against them, the Klan gained yet more support. The bombing of houses, and the injuring or even murder of African Americans, continued as many white Americans were afraid of the growing **civil rights** movement in the 1950s.

Brown versus Topeka Board of Education, 1954

In 1896, the US **Supreme Court** had decided that segregated (separate) schools were legal so long as they were equal. In most cases, they were not. Schools for white children were better funded than those for African American children. In 1954, twenty states had segregated schools. The **NAACP** challenged this inequality, and chose to base its case on the situation in Topeka in Kansas.

In May 1954, the Supreme Court unanimously declared that segregated schools were illegal under the US constitution. In 1955, the Supreme Court ruled that all states had to carry out the policy of desegregating their schools. Many southern states objected, and either did nothing or moved very slowly. Very little had happened by the end of 1956.

> ## Revision tasks
>
> 1 Summarise in your own words what **Source 1** on page 131 says.
>
> 2 Explain the implications of this decision by the Supreme Court – for education and for other aspects of life.

Key terms

Segregation: keeping a group separate from the rest of society, usually on the basis of race or religion. Segregation was seen in separate schools, transport and housing.
Jim Crow: the name Jim Crow was made popular by a white American comedian who made fun of African Americans. Originally, Jim Crow was a character in an old song. This name became linked to the southern laws ensuring that African American people remained inferior.

Key terms

Civil rights: legal rights, such as freedom of speech and the right to a fair trial. Most African Americans lacked these basic rights in the 1950s.
Supreme Court: a court of nine judges who decide on legal issues. The judges were appointed for life by the President.
NAACP: the National Association for the Advancement of Coloured People. This organisation fought for the rights of African Americans.

Rosa Parks and the Montgomery bus boycott, 1955–56

- In December 1955, Rosa Parks, aged 42, refused to give up her seat on a bus to a white person in Montgomery in Alabama.
- She was arrested and fined $10.
- African American people, encouraged by a young minister, Martin Luther King, started a bus boycott. They would walk to work.
- The boycott was very damaging to the bus company as African Americans made up about 75 per cent of the passengers.
- In spite of being made fun of in the streets by white people, African Americans remained calm and dignified. They did not fight back, even when Martin Luther King's house was bombed.
- In November 1956, the Supreme Court ruled that segregation on buses was illegal.
- In December 1956, the bus company gave in.
- Other bus companies in the southern states were slow to change their racist policy. White attitudes were deeply entrenched.

SOURCE 1

The Supreme Court decision, May 1954. These are the words of the Chief Justice, Earl Warren:

To separate black children from others of similar age and qualifications, solely because of their race, generates a feeling of inferiority as to their status in the community that may affect their hearts and minds in a way never to be undone … We conclude that in the field of public education the doctrine of 'separate but equal' has no place. Separate educational facilities are inherently unequal.

Revision tasks

1 Summarise in your own words what **Source 2** says about Martin Luther King's beliefs.

SOURCE 2

Martin Luther King's policy of non-violence. This is taken from a speech in Montgomery in 1955.

One of the great glories of democracy is the right to protest for right. There will be no crosses burned at any bus stops in Montgomery. There will be no white persons pulled out of their homes and taken out on some distant road and murdered … If you protest courageously and yet with dignity and Christian love, when the history books are written in future generations, the historians will pause and say, 'There lived a great people – a black people – who injected new meaning and dignity into the veins of civilisation'. That is our challenge and our overwhelming responsibility.

2 Explain the implications of this speech for:
- the Montgomery bus boycott
- future campaigns to achieve racial equality.

Comment

The nine African American students involved in the Little Rock High School incident were invited by Barack Obama to his inauguration as US President in January 2009.

Little Rock High School, Arkansas, 1957

- Little progress towards desegregating schools had been made by 1957.
- In 1957, nine African American students registered to attend Little Rock Central High School.
- The state governor, Orval Faubus, who was against integration, posted members of the National Guard (the reserve army in the USA) outside the school to prevent the African American students entering.
- National television showed film of the events outside the school, with an angry white mob jeering and jostling.
- Eventually, the African American students entered the school through a back door.
- President Eisenhower was forced to send federal troops to enforce the law that entitled these students to attend.
- Inside the school, these students continued to be the subject of abuse from many white students.

Exam practice

1 Explain the importance of events at Little Rock High School in 1957.
   (8 marks)

Exam tip For Exam practice question 1 above, you should aim to explain two or three factors (with some details) in order to reach the top level in the mark scheme.

The attitudes of many white Americans became even more extreme, determined not to give in to moves towards racial equality. Membership of the Ku Klux Klan grew. In many people's eyes, Governor Faubus was a hero. He remained as Governor of the state until 1967, though he had modified his views by the end of his period in office.

Moves in other schools towards racial integration progressed very slowly. However, a civil rights movement was developing, with support from both African and white Americans. It had some success – for example, in restaurants – but in other areas of life there was little evidence of change.

The living standards of African Americans

Living standards had improved a little compared with before the Second World War. However, in addition to unequal legal status, African Americans still had many of the worst paid jobs and had to work under the worst conditions. In 1957, the average income of an African American worker was 57 per cent of that of a white worker. Unemployment for African Americans was twice that for white Americans.

> **Exam tip** In all aspects of this study on American civil rights, you must try to understand the arguments and reasons given by **both** sides – not just the one you agree with!

13.2 How effective were the methods used by members of the civil rights movement between 1961 and 1968?

The 1960s was a period in the civil rights movement that saw rapid changes in tactics and in the level of success achieved. In 1961, the new President, John F. Kennedy, made it clear that he was a supporter of desegregation.

The freedom rides, 1961

Many states were not putting into effect the Supreme Court ruling about desegregating bus services.

- Groups of activists (mostly African American, but with some white supporters) rode on buses in the Birmingham, Alabama area to highlight the issue.
- They gained the name of 'freedom riders' – and were the subject of a lot of racial abuse and violence from white groups.
- There were 60 freedom rides, many crossing state boundaries, which involved 450 people.
- Two hundred freedom riders were arrested and put in jail.
- Eventually, the Governor of Alabama acted to protect the freedom riders after pressure from the new US President, Kennedy. In his opening speech as President, Kennedy had made it clear that he would support moves towards equality.
- It was made clear that the law against segregation applied to interstate buses (that is, buses that crossed state boundaries) as well as local ones.
- Through the new medium of television, civil rights had become a national issue.

> **Comment**
>
> *Remember that television footage of these events was seen across the USA. The pictures may only have been seen in black and white, but the violence shocked many citizens. Newspapers also carried photos and reports that showed the extent of the brutality.*

Freedom marches, 1963

By 1963, Martin Luther King and other civil rights leaders were keen to keep up the momentum of change. The city of Birmingham in Alabama had not changed any of its segregation policies, and King wanted to capture the media's attention. Therefore, he organised a series of freedom marches in the city.

- The head of police in Birmingham, Bull Connor, was racist and hot-headed. He would react badly to any African American attempts to gain sympathy.
- The police instructed the marchers to stop, but they refused.
- Television cameras were present as police and fire officers used dogs and fire hoses against peaceful marchers, who included men, women and children.

- Over 1,000 protesters were arrested and many, including King, put in jail.
- Nationally, public opinion was outraged. Birmingham was forced to desegregate.
- However, many white Americans felt betrayed by the Federal Government, and there were outbreaks of violence in the following months. For example, in September 1963, a bomb planted by Ku Klux Klan members killed four African American children in a Birmingham church.
- Over the country as a whole, there were many marches and demonstrations in more than 100 cities.

SOURCE 3

Extract from a letter written by Martin Luther King while he was in jail in Birmingham in 1963. You will see that the style of writing is interesting, with King building up a sense of outrage before he gets to his last point.

When you have seen vicious mobs lynch your mothers and fathers at will and drown your brothers and sisters on a whim; when you have seen hate-filled policemen curse, kick and even kill your black brothers and sisters; when you see the vast majority of your twenty million Negro brothers smothering in an airtight cage of poverty in the midst of an affluent society; when you are harried by day and haunted by night by the fact that you are a Negro; when you are forever fighting a degenerating sense of nobodiness; then you will understand why we find it difficult to wait.

Revision tasks

1 List the racial abuses that King refers to in **Source 3** and write a sentence about each.

2 Explain the point King makes at the end of the extract.

The Washington march, 1963

In August 1963, the most famous demonstration organised by Martin Luther King took place. It was intended to put pressure on President Kennedy's Government to move further in the direction of civil rights for all, including African Americans.

A quarter of a million people marched to the federal capital, Washington DC. Having arrived in Washington at dawn on 28 August, they met at the Washington Monument. At 11.30a.m. they marched to the Lincoln Memorial. Both these sites had special significance – named after the first US President and the President who ended slavery. Martin Luther King gave his famous speech – 'I have a dream'.

SOURCE 4

Part of Martin Luther King's speech.

I have a dream that one day this nation will rise up and live out the true meaning of its creed: we hold these truths to be self-evident, that all men are created equal. I have a dream that one day on the red hills of Georgia, the sons of former slaves and the sons of former slave owners will be able to sit down together at the table of brotherhood.
I have a dream that one day even the state of Mississippi, a state sweltering with the heat of injustice [and] oppression will be transformed into an oasis of freedom and justice.
I have a dream that my four little children will one day live in a nation where they will not be judged by the colour of their skin but by the content of their character.

Comment

You can watch the entire speech on the internet, search for 'Martin Luther King 'I have a dream' video'. Notice the deep emotion of the occasion on the part of Martin Luther King and his vast audience.

133

SOURCE 5

A photograph taken in Washington DC on 28 August 1963, showing the civil rights march on Washington.

Revision tasks

1 Study what **Source 4** on page 133 is saying, and write a summary in your own words.

2 Using **Sources 4** on page 133 and **5** on the left and your own knowledge, explain why so much progress had been made towards civil rights by the end of 1963.

In November 1963, President Kennedy was assassinated, but by then the issue of civil rights was high on the agenda for Government action.

The Black Power movement in the 1960s

Various African Americans became famous during the development of the Black Power movement, especially Stokely Carmichael and Malcolm X.

Martin Luther King believed in non-violence, and progress towards equality was gradually being made. However, even on key issues, such as voting, this progress was slow. Many African Americans, because of their own ignorance of what to do, or because of local restrictions, were not registered to vote.

	1960	1966
Texas	35%	80%
Arkansas	37%	54%
Louisiana	30%	42%
Mississippi	5%	28%
Alabama	15%	49%
Virginia	24%	44%

Percentage of African Americans registered to vote in some of the southern states of the USA.

Even though, as the table above shows, progress in voting rights for African Americans was being made, some people thought a more violent approach would bring quicker results. The Black Power movement developed during the mid-1960s at a time when progress on civil rights was being made through legal reforms (see pages 135–36). The Black Power movement wanted to increase awareness of African American culture; it wanted African Americans to be proud of their African roots.

Stokely Carmichael favoured this more direct approach, using violence when it was thought to be necessary. He became president of the Black Panther Party, which had been set up to promote Black Power and self-defence. This organisation also stirred up hatred of the Vietnam War at a time when most white Americans supported the USA's involvement.

SOURCE 6

The views of Malcolm X.

*I don't go along with any kind of non-violence unless everybody's going to be non-violent. If they make the Ku Klux Klan non-violent, I'll be non-violent. If they make the White Citizens' Council non-violent, I'll be non-violent. But as long as you've got somebody else not being non-violent, I don't want anybody coming to me talking any non-violent talk.
You get freedom by letting your enemy know that you'll do anything to get your freedom; then you'll get it. Fight them, and you'll get your freedom.*

Revision task

Compare the content of **Source 6** with the views of Martin Luther King.

The Black Panthers reacted angrily at what they saw as police brutality against African Americans – for example, in the Watts riots of 1965 in Los Angeles (see page 136). Violence was seen as a legitimate tactic against white supremacists. The Black Panthers had many clashes with the police, and several policemen were killed.

Malcolm X became a Muslim when in prison for drug-dealing and burglary. He led the Black Muslim Organisation. He wanted all African Americans to become Muslims. He saw Martin Luther King's policy of non-violence as weak, and he wanted to use violence to attack racism by white Americans who were usually closely identified with Protestantism. His own parents had been murdered by the Ku Klux Klan. He, too, was murdered in 1965, but by an African American gunman.

Black Power protests at the Mexico Olympic Games, 1968

Tommie Smith and John Carlos, African American sprinters, came first and third respectively in the 200-metres race. It was no surprise that they won medals, but what happened at the medal ceremony was a shock.

They went on the podium in black socks and no shoes. One wore a black scarf and the other black beads. They did a Black Power salute with a clenched fist in the air. At the end of the ceremony, the athletes were booed. Their actions were criticised by many Americans for bringing internal American politics into the Olympic Games.

13.3 How important was Martin Luther King in the fight for civil rights in the USA?

Martin Luther King's role as a protest organiser, 1955–63

Before Rosa Parks' arrest in December 1955 (see page 131), Martin Luther King had been working as a pastor at the Dexter Avenue Baptist Church in Montgomery. He became well-known beyond his congregation when he helped to organise the non-violent bus boycott.

As a result of this, he became a national figure in the civil rights movement during the next few years, leading up to the famous 'I have a dream' speech in Washington DC in August 1963 (pages 131–35).

Revision task

Look back over the earlier pages of this chapter (and use your own knowledge) to compile a list of events and activities with which Martin Luther King was involved, and note what each achieved.

Events and activities	What was achieved

The Civil Rights Act, 1964

Civil rights were an important national issue at the time of President Kennedy's assassination in November 1963. The new President, Lyndon Johnson, a Texan from the south of the USA, made it clear that he would support voting reform. Although, in theory, African American people could vote, in practice many were disqualified by local laws.

Comment

It is important that you try to understand those African Americans who believed that violence was the best way forward. Progress under non-violence had been slow. The younger generation of African Americans expected more to be achieved.

Exam practice

1 What effects did the violent Black Power groups have on the development of the civil rights movement?

(8 marks)

Exam tip For Exam practice question 1 above, you should aim to explain two or three consequences (with some details) in order to reach the top level in the mark scheme.

Comment

It is important that you try, as far as possible, to put Martin Luther King's achievements in the context of what was happening at the time. There were other leaders and groups promoting social change. King was not the only leader – but he gained the most attention, and was recognised not just within the USA, but in the rest of the world.

In July 1964, the Civil Rights Act was passed. This meant that:

- Racial discrimination was outlawed in employment, entertainment, and government agencies.
- Schools had to be desegregated if they were to receive any public funding.
- Only private clubs and other private organisations could be 'whites only'.
- An Equal Employment Opportunity Commission was set up to investigate complaints.

This was followed up in 1965 with the Voting Rights Act, which stopped racial discrimination in terms of voting. All local state restrictions for African Americans became illegal. In 1967, the Supreme Court ruled that any state laws forbidding mixed marriages were unconstitutional.

Another Civil Rights Act in 1968 concerned housing. It ruled that nobody could refuse to sell or rent a house to someone on the grounds of colour or race. Nor could house advertisements refer to colour or race.

Winning the Nobel Peace Prize, 1964

Martin Luther King received this award for his non-violent approach towards tackling racial inequality. At the time he was just 35 years old – the youngest man to have received the Nobel Peace Prize.

During the presentation speech in Oslo, Norway, in December 1964, it was said that: 'Luther King's name will endure for the way in which he has waged his struggle, personifying in his conduct the words that were spoken to mankind: "Whoever shall smite thee on thy right cheek, turn to him the other also!"'

Race riots, 1965–67

The Civil Rights Act of 1964 promised much, but many African Americans were becoming impatient, partly influenced by the Black Power movement.

In 1965, Martin Luther King organised marches in areas that had the worst record for continuing racial discrimination. He was concerned to get voting rights for all African Americans, but only 2.4 per cent of those in Selma, Alabama, were registered to vote. Organised marches from Selma to Montgomery were stopped brutally by the police with the use of tear gas and whips.

King was keen to avoid more brutality – as was President Johnson who pushed through the Voting Rights Act (1965) as quickly as possible.

However, racial troubles were not confined to the southern states. By 1965, 50 per cent of African Americans lived in the north of the USA. Many suffered from slum housing, high unemployment, poorly-paid jobs, poor education and much ill-health. African American babies were twice as likely to die as white babies. Local government and the police were always under white control. Here, in overcrowded cities, it was easy for situations to arise that led to violence.

In August 1965, violence erupted in the Watts area of Los Angeles. It was an African American ghetto, and white police officers had allegedly subjected some African Americans to unnecessary violence. Thirty-four people were killed in the riots and hundreds injured. Four thousand people were arrested.

Unfortunately, this sparked off riots elsewhere. In 1966, there were riots in Chicago after Martin Luther King had tried to help African Americans get better treatment from the city government. King was no longer able to control situations and persuade African Americans to be patient and non-violent.

In 1967, there were race riots in many North American cities. Eighty-three people died, most of them African Americans. Large areas of cities such as Detroit were looted and burned. President Johnson was horrified by the violence and set up a commission to investigate the causes. The report mostly blamed white racist attitudes causing anger in African American communities. White Americans still tended to put the blame on African American 'lawlessness' and demand tougher penalties.

> ## Exam practice
>
> 1 'The passing of the Civil Rights Act in 1964 meant that Martin Luther King had achieved his goals.' How far do you agree with this interpretation? Explain your answer.
>
> *(12 marks)*

> **Exam tip** In Exam practice question 1 above, you need to think of what King's aims were, and consider how much they had been achieved in practice. In particular, consider the fact that passing a law does not change people's attitudes overnight!

SOURCE 7

Attitudes of African Americans towards violence and non-violence at this time.

Years	Can win rights without violence	Violence was probably necessary
1963	63%	22%
1966	59%	21%
1970	58%	31%

Age groups in 1970	Can win rights without violence	Violence was probably necessary
14–21	55%	40%
22–29	58%	31%
30–49	55%	33%
50+	65%	20%

Statistics for 1970	African Americans as % of the population	African Americans as a % of the police force
Atlanta	38	10
Chicago	27	17
Detroit	39	5
Newark	40	10
Washington DC	63	21

> ### Revision task
> How useful are the statistics in **Source 7** in helping to explain the growing violence of the 1960s?

The assassination of Martin Luther King

By 1968, Martin Luther King had become a controversial figure. Many citizens, both African American and white, still regarded him as a hero in the struggle for civil rights. However, some people had ceased to support him because they believed that faster progress would be made by using violent methods. Others, both African American and white, criticised him for his opposition to the Vietnam War, which was reaching its height at this time. The Government saw him as a troublemaker, and his telephone conversations were tapped by the Federal Bureau of Investigation (FBI).

In March 1968, King was invited to Memphis, Tennessee, to support a strike by African American refuse collectors. He led a march that turned into violence and, disappointed, he went home to Atlanta. However, in April he returned to Memphis. The speech he made the night before his assassination has become famous.

SOURCE 8

From Martin Luther King's speech in Memphis, 3 April 1968.

Like anybody, I would like to live a long life. But I am not concerned about that now. I just want to do God's will. And He's allowed me to go up to the mountain. And I've looked over and I've seen the promised land. I may not get there with you. But I want you to know tonight that we as a people will get to the promised land. And I'm happy tonight. I'm not worried about anything. I'm not fearing any man. Mine eyes have seen the glory of the coming of the Lord.

The next day, as King stood on his motel balcony, he was assassinated by James Earl Ray, a white American. Unfortunately, this led to another outbreak of riots across America, as King's supporters bitterly accused white Americans of murdering their leader.

Revision tasks

1 Study **Source 8** on page 137, where Martin Luther King appears to be comparing himself with Moses, who led the Israelites out of Egypt. Use it to complete the following table.

Moses	Martin Luther King
The Israelites were slaves in Egypt.	
Moses was sent by God to free the Israelites.	
Moses led the slaves out of Egypt.	
The Israelites followed Moses through the wilderness.	
Moses led the Israelites to the Promised Land.	
Moses was shown the Promised Land before he died.	

2 Compile two lists – one of Martin Luther King's achievements for civil rights, and one of other people or events that contributed to what was achieved.

Study **Source 8** on page 137

Exam practice

1 'Martin Luther King was the most important factor in the civil rights movement, 1945–68.' How far do you agree with this interpretation? Explain your answer.

(12 marks)

Exam tip Exam practice question 1 above is a typical style of essay question used in the exams. First, prepare an answer in brief note form, jotting down reasons to agree and reasons to disagree. Then think how you can develop your ideas into longer arguments. Finally, consider what conclusion you might reach about the interpretation.

Key content

You need to have a good working knowledge of the following areas.
Tick off each item once you are confident in your knowledge.

- ❏ African American soldiers' experience of war
- ❏ Racial inequality in the USA after the Second World War; Segregation Laws
- ❏ Attitudes in the southern states and the Ku Klux Klan
- ❏ Education: *Brown v. Topeka Board of Education*; Little Rock High School
- ❏ Living standards for African Americans in the 1950s
- ❏ The civil rights movement: freedom rides; freedom marches
- ❏ The Washington march, 1963
- ❏ The Black Power movement in the 1960s; protests at the Mexican Olympics
- ❏ The role of Martin Luther King as a protest organiser, 1955–1963
- ❏ The Civil Rights Act, 1964
- ❏ Martin Luther King winning the Nobel Peace Prize, 1964
- ❏ The race riots of 1965–1967
- ❏ The assassination of Martin Luther King and its consequences

Check your knowledge online with our Quick quizzes at www.hodderplus.co.uk/modernworldhistory.

In the 1950s, the French were defeated and withdrew from Vietnam. In the 1960s, successive US presidents committed their armed forces to involvement in the conflict in Vietnam and supported South Vietnam in its attempts to stop a Communist invasion from the North. US tactics against the Vietcong forces did not work and brought much opposition at home. This, in turn, led to a gradual reduction in US involvement in the late 1960s and early 1970s. Eventually, the North triumphed and reunited Vietnam under Communist leadership.

Key issues

As with all examination topics, you will be expected to do more than simply learn the content and write it out again. You will need to show understanding of key issues from the period. These are:

- How effective were guerrilla tactics during the Vietnam War?
- How did the coverage of the Vietnam War in the USA lead to demands for peace?
- Why were the US actions to end the Vietnam War unsuccessful?

14.1 How effective were guerrilla tactics during the Vietnam War?

Developments in Vietnam before 1964

1. US involvement before 1954

Vietnam was part of the French empire until its occupation by the Japanese during the Second World War. Japan was defeated in 1945 and Vietnam was returned to the French. However, the Communist leader Ho Chi Minh opposed French control and declared Vietnam's independence in September 1945. This led to war between the French and supporters of Ho Chi Minh. The US President, Harry Truman, gave $3 million to support the French. This was due to American fears of the spread of Communism.

The Battle of Dien Bien Phu, 1954, and its consequences

The area we know as Vietnam had been a French colony before the Second World War, when it was occupied by the Japanese. After the war, the French wanted to reassert their rule. However, Vietminh guerrillas based in the northern area of Vietnam had become organised. They were led by Ho Chi Minh who was communist in sympathy, but he was supported by people with very different political opinions who all wanted to secure their independence from foreign domination.

By the early 1950s, the French controlled most cities and the Vietnamese nationalists controlled much of the countryside. The USA supported the French with large amounts of money. However, the countries had different motives. The French were fighting to preserve their empire; the Americans were fighting against Communism, and were strongly suspicious of Ho Chi Minh's communist sympathies. President Eisenhower refused a French request to send in US aircraft manned by American crews. The French were finding it difficult to make advances in the countryside against guerrilla tactics; the Vietminh did not have enough strength or firepower to attack the defensive French positions.

In 1954, the French decided to have a showdown at a place called Dien Bien Phu. It controlled the main routes between Vietnam and the neighbouring regions of Laos and Cambodia. The French built a fortified defensive position. The Vietminh guerrillas besieged the fortress. The French believed that their superior firepower would ensure victory. Instead, the Vietminh attacked and attacked, regardless of casualties. Eventually Vietminh units broke through the French defences.

The French had suffered 4,000 killed and wounded and 8,000 missing, mostly taken as prisoners. The Vietminh had 8,000 killed and 12,000 wounded. This battle ended French plans for holding on to their empire in the East. The Americans had provided a lot of financial help but not enough, and soon, as some French politicians predicted, became drawn into the area themselves.

At the Geneva peace conference, the following was decided:
- Vietnam would be temporarily divided into two along the 17th parallel (see map).
- The North would be under the control of the Communist regime of Ho Chi Minh.
- The South would be controlled by Ngo Dinh Diem, an anti-Communist Catholic politician.
- There would be a general election in 1956 for the whole of Vietnam to decide its future.

2. US support, 1954–60

The USA was determined to support South Vietnam against any possible takeover from the North. This was due to the domino theory – the USA feared that, one by one, each country in Asia would fall to Communism, like a row of dominoes. American support for South Vietnam included:
- $1.6 billion in aid between 1954 and 1960
- sending US military advisers in 1954 to help 'prepare' for the 1956 elections
- backing Diem's refusal to hold elections in 1956 in case the Communists won.

Diem's corrupt Government became very unpopular. Leading Socialists, Communists, journalists and trade unionists were arrested. Buddhists were excluded from top government positions. In the villages, the traditionally elected councils were replaced by Saigon officials.

The National Liberation Front (NLF) was set up in opposition to Diem and soon controlled parts of the countryside in South Vietnam. It was given supplies and support from Ho Chi Minh and wanted to reunite North and South and to introduce economic and social reform.

3. US involvement during the Kennedy years, 1961–63

Kennedy did not like Diem, but was determined to prevent the spread of Communism from the North. The NLF, now known as the Vietcong or VC, had grown to 16,000 members. The USA tried to counter its influence by:

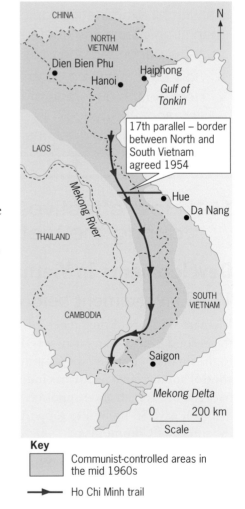

17th parallel – border between North and South Vietnam agreed 1954

Key

Communist-controlled areas in the mid 1960s

Ho Chi Minh trail

- sending even more military advisers – by 1962, there were 11,000 training the South Vietnamese army, known as the ARVN
- the 'strategic hamlets' policy in which hamlets supporting the Vietcong were moved and replaced by new ones defended by barbed wire and the ARVN. This policy did not work as many South Vietnamese resented having to move. It increased support for the Vietcong.

Diem's unpopularity grew. He imprisoned and killed hundreds of Buddhists, who he claimed were helping the Communists. Some Buddhist monks burned themselves in protest. Diem's anti-Buddhist policy lost him the support of the USA, and in November 1963 he was assassinated by his army generals.

The theory of guerrilla warfare

The Vietcong copied the methods that had been used successfully by the communists in China in the decades before Mao Zedong came to power in 1949. This involved using **guerrilla tactics** because the Vietcong knew that they could not hope to defeat the USA in open battle. Instead, Vietcong soldiers came out of hiding, attacked US equipment and personnel, and rapidly retreated. The Vietcong also worked hard to win the support of the people of South Vietnam by befriending them and portraying the Americans as foreign invaders.

Guerrilla tactics, 1964–68

- Guerrilla tactics were ideal in jungle conditions. The Vietcong were able to make booby traps, carry out ambushes and sabotage US bases, and then disappear into the jungle. As most of the population supported the Vietcong, it was almost impossible to detect them in the villages.
- The Vietcong built thousands of kilometres of tunnels and complex underground shelters to avoid US air raids and reduce casualties. Often US troops were killed by booby traps.
- The Vietcong had much support in the villages, and those who did not support them were terrorised into providing shelter and food.
- The Vietcong was supplied by the North Vietnamese via the **Ho Chi Minh Trail**. Other Communist countries, such as the USSR and China, gave at least 6,000 tonnes of supplies per day to North Vietnam to fight the USA.

> **Key term**
>
> **Guerrilla tactics:** hit-and-run tactics against an enemy that is more powerful in terms of weapons than if they were to meet in a face-to-face battle.

> **Key term**
>
> **Ho Chi Minh Trail:** a series of trails, often through dense jungles and crossing mountains and rivers, from North Vietnam to the South. Many of the trails passed through neutral Cambodia and Laos. They could be usd by trucks as well as people on foot or cycle.

The Vietcong tunnel system.

> **SOURCE 1**
>
> An American view of South Vietnam taken from a report written in 1964 by the US Secretary of Defence, Robert McNamara.
>
> *We seek an independent, non-Communist South Vietnam. We do not require South Vietnam to serve as a western base or become a member of the western alliance. South Vietnam must be free to accept outside assistance in order to maintain its security.*

The US response to guerrilla tactics

1. Operation Rolling Thunder, 1965

The Vietcong were receiving a lot of support from North Vietnam, and various incidents provided excuses for the USA to launch attacks there.

In 1964, the Gulf of Tonkin incident was used as an excuse by the new President, Lyndon Johnson, to take action against North Vietnam. It was claimed that North Vietnamese patrol boats had attacked the US destroyer, the *Maddox*, in the Gulf of Tonkin. The USA responded with a bombing raid.

In 1965, a more serious incident occurred. The Vietcong attacked an American base at Pleiku. Nine Americans were killed and nearly 100 wounded. The USA responded with a major bombing of North Vietnam, code-named Operation Rolling Thunder.

This operation was designed to destroy roads, railways and Vietcong bases in North Vietnam, and especially the Ho Chi Minh Trail – the supply route from North to South Vietnam for the Vietcong.

Saturation bombing did not flush out or destroy the Vietcong. It had little effect against the guerrilla tactics used by the Vietcong. By the end of 1965, there were 180,000 US troops in South Vietnam, but the Vietcong had not been defeated.

2. 'Hearts and minds'

At the same time as using military strength to try to bomb North Vietnam into submission, the USA spent money and materials trying to help ordinary South Vietnamese people – for example, improving roads, building schools and establishing health clinics.

This policy had some success in the towns and cities in winning over 'hearts and minds'. However, in the rural areas the Vietcong had much more influence and support. This factor became increasingly important in the guerrilla warfare of the late 1960s.

3. Search-and-destroy

The Americans used search-and-destroy tactics to try to flush the Vietcong out of the countryside. They used helicopters that landed close to Vietcong-controlled villages in the hope of getting into the village before the Vietcong could arm themselves. This was not easy because:

- It was difficult to distinguish the Vietcong from the normal Vietnamese people.
- The US soldiers found the conditions very difficult due to the heat, the jungle and the mosquitoes.

Civilian casualties in search-and-destroy raids were very high. This made the US and South Vietnamese forces even more unpopular with the peasants. Often excessive brutality was used to try to get information from villagers about the Vietcong. If Vietcong suspects were found, whole villages were destroyed.

4. Agent Orange and napalm

The Americans decided to use chemical weapons to try to flush the Vietcong out of the jungles. These weapons included:

- Agent Orange, which destroyed hundreds of thousands of hectares of forest and crops. Exposure to Agent Orange caused cancers, birth defects, etc. Both the Vietnamese peasants and the US forces were affected
- napalm, an incendiary weapon which contained petrol, chemicals and phosphorous, and burned the skin right to the bone.

These tactics did not work. As well as destroying much of the countryside and killing and wounding thousands of civilians, they:

Revision task

In your own words, explain the views expressed in **Source 1** on page 141 and **Source 2** above.

Comment

By the end of the Vietnam War, more bombs had been dropped on North Vietnam than on Germany and Japan combined throughout the Second World War.

Comment

As a result of American chemical warfare, there are still many Vietnamese alive today who were born with physical defects caused by chemicals that entered the water supply. Over 2 million hectares of forest were destroyed by chemicals.

- turned world opinion against the USA for using such inhumane weapons
- alienated even more of the population of South Vietnam, who turned to the Vietcong.

American tactics evolved and changed during the course of the war in Vietnam, from saturation bombing, to search-and-destroy missions, and the use of chemical weapons. None of these was successful in defeating the Vietcong. Indeed, in most respects, they had the opposite effect. They alienated the people of Vietnam and increased their support for the Vietcong.

The My Lai massacre, 1968

In March 1968, US forces under the command of Lieutenant William Calley entered the village of My Lai, which was suspected of hiding Vietcong troops. In a few hours, between 300 and 500 unarmed civilians, many of them women and children, were killed. It was the worst of many cases of inhuman US behaviour towards the South Vietnamese.

The incident only became known when one of the soldiers gave an account of the events on American television in 1969. This led to an official investigation. When the results of the investigation were published, the American public was shocked. Americans were revolted to learn how innocent civilians had been cruelly butchered. This, more than any other factor, turned American public opinion against the war.

Comment

Lieutenant Calley was put on trial and sentenced in 1970 to life imprisonment with hard labour. In fact, he was released in 1974.

Revision task

Using **Sources 3** and **4** and your own knowledge, describe Communist tactics in Vietnam against the US forces.

Exam practice

1 Explain the effect of American tactics in Vietnam on the attitudes of Vietnamese civilians.

(8 marks)

Exam tip For Exam practice question 1, you should aim to explain two or three causes/consequences/factors (with some details) in order to reach the top level in the mark scheme.

SOURCE 3

The aims of the North Vietnamese. This is taken from a letter written in 1965 by a member of Ho Chi Minh's Government. It was written in response to the large-scale arrival of US forces in 1965.

We need to use the methods most suited for destroying the American troops – guerrilla forces encircling the American troops' bases.
This upcoming spring and summer we are aiming for killing about 10,000 Americans as already planned, and for the next few years we should at least kill 40,000 to 50,000 Americans. This is a new goal which will determine our victory. The more troops the US brings in, the more military bases it builds. The larger area it occupies, the more sophisticated weapons it uses, the more B-52 bombs it drops, the more chemical poisons it uses, the worse the conflict between our people and them become; the more our people hate them.

SOURCE 4

A Vietcong poster from the 1960s.

SOURCE 5

US tactics in Vietnam. From an account by Sergeant James Weeks, a US soldier fighting in Vietnam, describing the orders he was given in 1967. From Malcolm Chandler and John Wright, *Modern World History for Edexcel.*

It was explained to us that anything alive in that area was supposed to be dead. We were told that if we saw a 'gook' (slang for Vietnamese person) or thought we saw one, no matter how big or small, shoot first. No need for permission to fire. It was just a turkey shoot – men, women and children, no matter what their ages, all went into the body count. This was a regular 'search-and-destroy' mission in which we destroyed everything we found.

14.2 How did the coverage of the Vietnam War in the USA lead to demands for peace?

Media coverage of the war

American TV reported the war fully – and in colour. It was the first television war. Radio, newspapers and television had a huge influence on attitudes towards the conflict. These attitudes were increasingly unfavourable. Some images have become famous – such as the execution of a Vietcong suspect with a gun pointed at his head, and the naked girl fleeing a napalm attack.

The influence of media coverage linked in with other reasons for opposing the war.

- From the start, some people had opposed American involvement in a war that they felt did not directly affect the USA.
- Martin Luther King opposed the war for this reason, and because of the disproportionate number of African American casualties. African Americans found it more difficult to avoid being called up than white Americans, and then were often in the most dangerous combat areas.
- Others believed that the USA was spending far too much money on the war – money that should be financing President Johnson's promised social reforms in the USA. Opposition grew when taxes were raised in 1967.
- The exposure of the My Lai massacre of 1968 in the following year led to even more opposition.
- The trial of Lieutenant Calley for the My Lai massacre reinforced opposition to what was happening in Vietnam. The guilty verdict was widely applauded, showing how much public opinion had moved against American involvement in the war. The USA's stated aim of preserving freedom and democracy seemed very false when faced with the evidence of My Lai.

Protest movements in the USA, 1968–73

Opposition to the war became organised by 1968, well before the My Lai revelations.

- Burning draft cards: men who were to be conscripted (drafted) into the army received a draft card. Some just refused to go. Others burned their draft card in public. Both were criminal offences, and by the end of 1969 there were 34,000 draft-dodgers wanted by the police. Many had escaped abroad – to Canada or beyond – to avoid arrest.
- Raiding draft board offices and burning the records held there: draft cards were sent out from these offices. In Catonsville, Maryland, two Catholic priests were imprisoned for being involved in these raids.
- Demonstrations and protest marches: in 1967, on placards in hugely supported marches, President Johnson had been publicly criticised as a war criminal. In 1968, he announced that he was not standing for re-election as President. In the summer of that year, 10,000 demonstrators went to Chicago to the Democratic Party Convention to protest against the war. Anti-war pressure was maintained during the presidential election campaign until Nixon had been voted in – promising to bring the war to an end.
- War veterans held marches: these men had been US soldiers who had fought in Vietnam, and many of them had been badly injured. Over 300,000 took part in a war veterans march in 1971.

The Kent State University protest, 1970

Many university students in the late 1960s and early 1970s protested on a wide range of issues – for example, in favour of **civil rights**. However, Vietnam became the main area of focus.

- Students held demonstrations and protests, usually peacefully, on university campuses and in nearby towns and cities.
- They went on strike in their universities.
- They burned their draft papers.
- They disrupted transport used for moving troops and army supplies.

The most famous protest was at Kent State University in Ohio in 1970. Over 1,000 students demonstrated and caused some damage. The National Guard was called in, and first used tear gas, and then bullets. Four students were shot dead and nine others were wounded.

This event was broadcast all over the USA and the world, causing reactions of shock and revulsion. It also had a big effect on the Government of President Nixon.

The Fulbright hearings, 1971

Within Congress, one of the two houses, the Senate, has a Foreign Affairs Committee. In 1971, its chairman was William Fulbright. The committee investigated the Vietnam War with a view to giving advice on how to end US involvement there.

As people gave evidence, more and more emerged about the inhuman behaviour of US troops in Vietnam. My Lai was not just an isolated incident. Such behaviour had been encouraged by the military leadership. The effect of these hearings was to raise questions at an official Government level about the purpose of US involvement in Vietnam.

Key term

Civil rights: legal rights, such as freedom of speech and the right to a fair trial.

Exam practice

1 Explain how the media in the USA influenced opinion about the Vietnam War.

(8 marks)

Exam tip For Exam practice question 1 above, you should aim to explain two or three factors (with some details) in order to reach the top level in the mark scheme.

SOURCE 6

An anti-war demonstration in Washington DC, 1967.

SOURCE 7

A shocked student holds her head in disbelief as she looks at the body of one of the four students shot dead at Kent State University, 1970.

14.3 Why were the US actions to end the Vietnam War unsuccessful?

The Tet Offensive, 1968

In 1968, the Vietcong launched a surprise offensive during the Tet (New Year) festival. They attacked 36 cities and even reached Saigon where, for a short period of time, they held the US embassy. They were eventually forced to retreat with very heavy losses. From now on, it was the North Vietnamese army that did most of the fighting, rather than the Vietcong.

In many respects, this was a military victory for the USA but, in the long term, it had a disastrous effect on the attitudes of Americans, especially witnessing their own embassy under attack, as well as the thousands of civilian casualties and thousands of refugees. World opinion was also turning against American involvement in Vietnam. It was at this time that President Johnson decided not to seek re-election.

Vietnamisation

The advances made by the Vietcong in the Tet Offensive so shocked the American public that President Richard Nixon (who took office in 1969) decided to introduce the policy of 'Vietnamisation'. This meant training the Vietnamese army to fight on its own using US arms and supplies, and withdrawing US troops. Between 1969 and 1971, about 400,000 troops were withdrawn.

The number of US troops in Vietnam was at this time only 150,000. These remaining soldiers were often pessimistic about their role. At the same time, the South Vietnamese army (the ARVN) was greatly expanded, to be trained and equipped by the USA.

US bombing of the North, Laos and Cambodia

At the time when Nixon became President in January 1969, it was becoming increasingly recognised that a peaceful solution should be sought. Talks had begun in Paris in 1968, and continued until 1973. This gives an indication of how difficult it was to make diplomatic progress. Basically, the USA demanded that South Vietnam should be an independent state, whereas North Vietnam wanted a united Communist country.

The USA continued to put pressure on North Vietnam by continuing the bombings. In addition, as North Vietnam was still supplying the Vietcong with weapons along the Ho Chi Minh Trail through Cambodia and Laos, Nixon ordered the bombing of these countries as well. In 1970, US troops entered Cambodia with the objective of destroying the trail.

In 1971 and 1972, there were renewed bombing attacks on North Vietnam, causing great destruction to ports, roads, railways and cities. This massive bombing slowed down the progress of the invasion from the North, which was happening in 1972 with the help of Soviet tanks.

The bombing of the North made both sides realise that a military solution was not imminent, and therefore the North Vietnamese agreed to resume talks in Paris in January 1973.

Comment

Ever since the early 1970s, unexploded bombs in Laos have continued to kill and injure people – there have been more than 12,000 deaths so far. More cluster bombs were dropped on Laos during the Vietnam War than on any other country in the world. International organisations are still working full time to clear unexploded bombs, using local trained experts, including women. Meanwhile, much fertile land is too dangerous to farm and roads are slow to be built.

Paris peace conference and US withdrawal, 1973

Agreement was reached at Paris on the terms for ending the war.
- All US armed forces would leave Vietnam.
- US prisoners of war were to be released by North Vietnam.
- The Government of South Vietnam continued to exist, but North Vietnamese forces could stay in areas of South Vietnam that they controlled.
- Elections to be held in the future would determine whether Vietnam became united or not.

All US troops had left Vietnam by April 1973. Only US advisers remained. The North Vietnamese were in a good position to complete the conquest of the South.

The fall of Saigon, 1975

In 1975, the North Vietnamese attacked South Vietnam via Cambodia and Laos as well as from North Vietnam. Major cities in South Vietnam quickly fell to the Communists. Many South Vietnamese troops retreated (or deserted) towards Saigon in the south.

In April 1975, Saigon fell to the Communists. Remaining US officials were airlifted by helicopter from the roof of the US embassy to be taken to nearby warships. Civilians had the choice of either accepting the Communists or fleeing from the capital, many of them escaping by boat.

Nearly 4 million Vietnamese had been killed or wounded in the war, 57,000 US troops died and over 300,000 had been wounded, many with permanent injuries.

The reasons for US defeat

1. Vietcong strengths

These were:
- the use of guerrilla warfare and a defensive system of underground tunnels
- working with and gaining the support of the people of South Vietnam
- an efficient supply line from the North along the Ho Chi Minh Trail
- assistance from China and the USSR
- skilful propaganda, portraying the US as foreigners interfering in South Vietnam.

2. US weaknesses

These were:
- tactics that seemed to lack coherence and clear planning
- unenthusiastic soldiers
- an inability to deal with the guerrilla tactics of the Vietcong
- alienating the South Vietnamese people through heavy-handed tactics
- difficulty in coping with the conditions in Vietnam, such as the jungle and heat
- the weakness of the army of South Vietnam.

3. The importance of public opinion

It is difficult to measure the impact of public opinion on the war.
- It influenced Nixon in his decision to introduce a policy of Vietnamisation.
- It badly affected the morale of new recruits as well as those fighting in Vietnam, many of whom did not understand US motives for involvement.
- On the other hand, more than half the US public generally supported the war.

SOURCE 8

Comments on the agreements reached at Paris in January 1973, made by a US intelligence adviser a few years later in 1978. From Chandler and Wright, *Modern World History for Edexcel.*

When we read the drafts of the agreement – what we were prepared to give as concessions to the North Vietnamese – it was clear that there was no way the Government of South Vietnam was going to be able to withstand Vietcong infiltration and propaganda before the election. Once I saw the concessions, I knew that we were prepared to sell South Vietnam down the river.

Revision task

Use the section on 'The reasons for US defeat', opposite and your own knowledge to consider the reasons for the defeat. Draw a spider diagram showing the main reasons. Then try to number each of your reasons in order of importance.

Next, write a paragraph to explain why each reason was important. Finally, number each of your paragraphs in order of importance.

Key content

You need to have a good working knowledge of the following areas. **Tick off each item** once you are confident in your knowledge.

- ❑ French defeat at Dien Bien Phu and its consequences
- ❑ US increasing involvement in the late 1950s and early 1960s
- ❑ The theory of guerrilla warfare in Vietnam; guerrilla tactics, 1964–1968
- ❑ The US policies of Operation Rolling Thunder and 'Hearts and Minds'
- ❑ Agent Orange and napalm; Search-and-Destroy
- ❑ The My Lai Massacre, 1968
- ❑ Media coverage of the Vietnam War, including the role of television
- ❑ Public reaction to the My Lai Massacre; the trial of Lieutenant Calley
- ❑ Protest movements in the USA, 1968–1973; the Kent State University protest, 1970
- ❑ The Fulbright Hearings, 1971
- ❑ The Tet Offensive and its impact on the war
- ❑ The US bombing of the North and attacks on Laos and Cambodia, 1970
- ❑ The Paris peace conference and US withdrawal, 1973
- ❑ The fall of Saigon, 1975

Check your knowledge online with our Quick quizzes at www.hodderplus.co.uk/modernworldhistory.

Exam practice

1 Explain the attitude of the US Government to the Paris peace talks in January 1973.
(8 marks)

2 'American public opinion was the main cause of US defeat in Vietnam.' How far do you agree with this interpretation? Explain your answer.
(12 marks)

Exam tip: q1 For Exam practice question 1 above, you should aim to explain two or three factors (with some details) in order to reach the top level in the mark scheme.

Exam tip: q2 In planning an answer to Exam practice question 2 above, list the reasons that allow you partly to agree with the interpretation. Then list the reasons that suggest other factors were also important. In your conclusion, try to evaluate how important American public opinion was in influencing the outcome of the war.